High Fiber
High Flavor

ROSEMARY MOON

High Fiber
High Flavor

More than 180 recipes for good health

FIREFLY BOOKS

A FIREFLY BOOK

Published by Firefly Books Ltd., 2000

First Printing

Canadian Cataloguing in Publication Data
Moon, Rosemary
High fiber, high flavor: more than 180 delicious recipes for good health
Includes index.
ISBN 1-55209-518-5
1. High-fiber diet – Recipes. I. Title
RM237.6.M66   2000   641.5'637   C99-932438-1

U.S. Cataloguing in Publication Data
Moon, Rosemary
High fiber, high flavor: more than 180 delicious recipes
for good health/Rosemary Moon.—1st ed.
[224] p. : col. ill. ; cm
Includes index.
ISBN 1-55209-518-5
1. High-fiber diet – Recipes. 2. Cookery. I. Title
641.563 -dc21   2000   CIP

First published in Canada in 2000 by
Firefly Books Ltd.
3680 Victoria Park Avenue
Willowdale, Ontario
M2H 3KI

First published in the United States in 2000 by
Firefly Books (U.S.) Inc.
P.O. Box 1338, Ellicott Station
Buffalo, New York 14205

FBPR
This book was conceived, designed, and produced by
Quintet Publishing Limited
6 Blundell Street
London N7 9BH

Project Editor: Laura Price
Art Director: Simon Daley
Editor: Anna Bennett
Designer: Paul Wright
Photographers: Ian Garlick and Andrew Sydenham
Food Stylists: Kathryn Hawkins and Rosemary Moon

Creative Director: Richard Dewing
Publisher: Oliver Salzmann

Typeset in Great Britain by
Central Southern Typesetters, Eastbourne
Manufactured in Hong Kong by Regent Publishing Services Ltd.
Printed in Singapore by Star Standard Industries Pte. Ltd.

Contents

6 Introduction

24 Soups and chowders

58 Salads and appetizers

98 Main dishes

148 Desserts

180 Breads, cakes and, cookies

222 Index

Introduction

Eating is one of the greatest pleasures in life for many of us privileged to live in relative security and affluence in the Western world. There is so much available to us; virtually every fruit and vegetable can be found fresh throughout the year on supermarket shelves, and almost all the ingredients for any style of national or international cuisine can be found without difficulty.

Life is made very easy for us. The drudgery and tedium has been removed from so many day-to-day jobs, allowing us more time to live life in the fast lane, to work full-time as well as run a home, to pursue hobbies, sports, and other leisure interests throughout the week and not just weekends. Everything is self-cleaning to allow us more time

and foods are being processed and prepared so that we simply have to heat them up.

It is the preparation of food for an easy life that particularly concerns me. Prepared and processed foods cut down dramatically on the time required to produce a meal but it is the things that are added to these foods, like additives and preservatives, and, more importantly, the things that are taken away, like bran and other forms of fiber, that should be carefully considered in terms of a balanced and healthy diet.

Not all processed food products are complete foods or convenience meals; white flour, which has had all the bran removed from it, is a

processed food and so is white rice, which has been polished to remove the outer husk, making it quicker to cook and easier to digest. White flour and refined sugar are good for baking, but the finished cake or bread has little nutritional value, except that it is high in fat and carbohydrates in the form of sugars and starch.

WHAT IS FIBER?

Fiber has become a buzzword of the modern age, prompted by growing concern about and awareness of a healthy diet. There is a certain amount of irony in this, however, as fiber used to be abundant in our diets and it is only through progress in food production and preparation, and affluence that we have started to remove it from our everyday foods. Now, we are beginning to suffer the consequences.

Dietary fiber is the substance that forms the cell walls of all plants – the superstructure or skeleton of the plant world. There is no dietary fiber in fish, meat, or dairy products; it is unique to plants and, as recently as the 1960s, was generally disregarded as being of no nutritional value. The milling and processing of foods was therefore a reasonable idea – getting rid of the tough outer coating to reveal a more attractive and easily digestible food.

Every age has common diseases and every set of circumstances poses problems regarding health. So many of the diseases that are now common in the Western world were far less prevalent in the past, and there is an obvious link between many intestinal disorders and the processed, soggy diet of our busy, affluent society. In the less developed countries of the world – where the staple diet of many is rice, lentils, and vegetables – there is also disease, but in many cases it is associated with vitamin deficiencies rather than with a lack of dietary fiber.

There is now significant evidence that a healthy diet – one rich in fiber – can help to prevent many of the so-called "modern diseases" that are especially linked with the digestive system, such as diabetes, gallstones, appendicitis, and disorders of the bowel, as well as heart disease. To keep as healthy an internal system as possible, it is important to cook with and eat as many unprocessed foods as possible. This leads us inevitably towards a high-fiber diet.

THE BASIC PRINCIPLES OF A HIGH-FIBER DIET

Eating a high-fiber diet is little more than common sense, a "back-to-nature" approach to eating. This means using fresh foods whenever possible, or frozen foods such as vegetables and prawns. It also means using basic products that have been processed as little as possible to maintain their fiber content.

The most obvious example of this is the milling of wheat and the production of flour. Once milling was an established mechanical process rather than being carried out by hand in small quantities between two stones, it became fashionable to eat white bread. This is made from flour that not only has been milled, but has had all the bran (the outer fibrous husk) sieved out of it. White bread was, and by many people still is, considered to be light, attractive in color, and soft to eat. Eventually, commercial steam bakeries were introduced, producing a moist, spongy white bread to be sliced and packed in plastic bags before sale. It seems to me that every last trace of fiber has been removed from such bread, as well as the ability to satisfy the appetite. Sure enough, for the devoted white bread eater, there are now commercial loaves with grains added to provide some dietary fiber, following the realization that fiber-rich foods are essential to a healthy modern diet; but a loaf made with whole-wheat flour must surely make a better choice of bread than that.

EATING FOR PLEASURE AND FOR HEALTH

I find the word "diet" can be off-putting. Eating is, for me, a great pleasure, the taste, texture, and combination of foods in any dish being the secret of a delicious meal. "Diet," with its connotations of weight reduction or a strict health regimen, implies deprivation. Eating healthily does not mean having to endure dull or unappetizing food. On the contrary, including fiber-rich foods in a healthy, modern diet is far more pleasurable than it sounds!

The secret of success when changing from one eating habit to another is to enjoy the challenge and to be motivated. A high-fiber way of life requires you to eat plenty of fruit and vegetables, less meat and dairy products, and more natural cereals, grains, and legumes. It is a regime that makes sense to anyone interested in health and the environment and, more importantly, to anyone interested in food and cooking.

AN INTRODUCTION TO HIGH-FIBER FOODS

There is a tendency to associate high-fiber foods almost exclusively with vegetarian cookery. This is an easy mistake, as the high-fiber diet is based on grains, cereals, beans, and legumes, all of which are vegetarian foods. These foods also serve to cut down on the amount of animal proteins that non-vegetarians eat and to provide more variety in our food.

It is important that we try to reduce the amount of meat and dairy products we consume, and combining these foods with others high in fiber provides a sensible and balanced diet.

Fresh fruit and vegetables contain significant amounts of fiber and should certainly be included in all eating regimes, not only for their fiber but also for their valuable vitamins and minerals. As a matter of taste (which is, after all, what eating is about for those of us who are not simply eating to

survive), many of us prefer our vegetables cooked, especially root vegetables such as potatoes and turnips, to make them more pleasant and more easily digestible. It is, however, a good idea to try to eat some raw foods every day – if you eat four different kinds of raw fruit, you will be doing well. Some vegetables, such as carrots and celery, make quick and easy snacks as an alternative to fruit. It is also good to get into the habit of eating a fresh salad every day.

TO PEEL OR NOT TO PEEL

To gain the maximum amount of dietary fiber from fruit and vegetables, you should eat them unpeeled. This is naturally a matter of taste, but it can also depend on where you buy your vegetables and how they are grown. Modern farming methods have become extremely reliant on pesticides, which often leave residues on the produce or in the soil. For the wonderful flavor of young carrots, freshly dug, washed, and steamed, go for organically grown produce.

In most of the recipes in this book, I have not specified whether vegetables and fruit should be peeled or not – that is a matter of individual preference. By all means peel carrots for carrot cake, but leave them whole for casseroles, risottos, and salads. If you do peel your vegetables, however, put the peelings to good use – they make an excellent flavoring for vegetable stock, but remember to strain the peelings from the stock before use.

Cereals and grains

These may sound like two completely separate groups of foods but they are really just one and the same. Grain is the fruit or seed of a cereal and it is a term frequently applied to wheat and other food-related grasses and their fruit or seeds. A cereal may be defined as being of wheat or another edible grain, and is also the name applied to foods that are made from grains, for example, breakfast cereals.

THE HISTORY OF GRAINS

Grains, the basic foodstuff of the world, really changed the face of civilization once humans set about cultivating them.

Early humans were nomadic and opportunistic eaters, hunting and adding wild fruit, berries, and plants to the basic diet. They traveled around, especially to look for grazing once they started to domesticate animals. Ancient forms of wheat and other grains grew in the wild and it was found that the seeds from these could be eaten. They became more palatable if the outer husks were removed and the grains ground between stones and mixed to a paste for baking. They also kept well, especially if picked when fully ripe and dry, and could therefore be stored.

It may well have been a chance discovery – a lucky accident that changed the life of early humans – when it was found that these grains, scattered over the land, would grow again, yielding another crop for another year. However, once humans made a conscious decision to grow grains, rather than just harvesting them when found by chance, it became necessary to stay in one place in order to nurture the crop and harvest it. So humans decided to abandon the nomadic life and, literally, put down roots.

STAPLE CROPS THROUGHOUT THE WORLD

Wheat and barley are known to have been the earliest crops and were grown throughout the early world in the Middle East. As humans traveled out across the continents, they took their early crops with them, and these grains became staple foods for early Chinese, Egyptian, and Indian peoples. All crops have their ideal growing conditions, and it became clear that, while these crops thrived in hot and sunny climates, they did not fare well in very wet areas. Other grains, however, such as oats, rye, and buckwheat, were successful and humans began to incorporate these in crops. It is thought that at first these crops may well have grown as weeds among wheat and barley, struggling in the warmer Mediterranean climate, but were eventually found to flourish in colder and wetter conditions.

Millet, a cereal that is not as common in Western cooking as in other cuisines, is extremely tolerant of high temperatures and grows well in Africa and Asia, where it can withstand very hot and dry, almost arid, conditions. Another grain that can withstand heat but must have plenty of moisture is rice, which is grown, half-submerged in water, in the paddy fields of China, India, and Southeast Asia. Rice is also grown in Italy, Spain, and North America, but in much smaller quantities. The countries that produce the majority of the world's rice are some of the most densely populated areas of the world, and rice remains the staple food of more than half the world's population.

ABOVE LEEK AND SPINACH BARLEY SOUP (SEE PAGE 56)

Maize, or corn, was one of the oldest crops in the Americas, but the original wild crop is thought to have died out many thousands of years ago. It must have been able to regenerate by self-sowing in the wild, but the modern corn kernel remains firmly and tightly attached to the cob, its natural carrier. Modern corn would not continue if it were not harvested from the cob and subsequently planted, by hand or machine. Although maize is most commonly found in Africa and the Americas, its indigenous home, it is now grown in some parts of Mediterranean Europe, especially in Italy and Spain, and also in China and India.

GRAINS AND CEREALS

Grains and cereals are the most important source of carbohydrates in the diet, but the amount of fiber yielded by them depends on the extent to which they have been processed. There are three parts to a grain: the outer husk, which is commonly known as the bran and contains most of the fiber; the endosperm, the largest part of the grain which contains most of the starch; and the germ, which contains the kernel or new growth of the plant, and therefore is the grain's source of protein. To benefit from the whole nutritional value of a cereal it is, therefore, essential to eat the whole grain. Milling not

B R O W N   R I C E

W I L D   R I C E

W H E A T

only removes the bran, it also take away nutrients such as vitamins B and E. Most cereals contain only around 1.5 percent fiber, but compared to other foods we regard them as high-fiber; this shows just how important it is to include them as whole grains in our diet.

Buy all grains and cereals in as natural, or unrefined, a form as possible. It is in the processing of grains that fiber may be lost, so it is important to know what to look for when buying potentially fiber-rich foods. For a high-fiber diet, you should always buy whole-wheat flour; this means that it is the whole of the edible grain, with all the bran – the fiber-rich part of the food.

STORING CEREALS AND GRAINS

As these are dry foods, they must be kept dry, either in storage canisters, jars, or tubs. Keep all dry goods on shelves rather than on the floor and use them in strict rotation, using the oldest first to avoid keeping very old stock. Even flour does not keep forever, and I find that whole-wheat flour is more inclined to become slightly rancid than white flour. Stone-ground flour does not keep as well as regular whole-wheat flour, although I think it has a finer texture and flavor. Even if you are a very keen baker and make all your own bread, you should not be tempted to buy flour in bulk quantities – the fresher the

better, so use it up quickly. I recommend keeping whole-wheat flour for no longer than six months.

COMMON VARIETIES OF CEREALS AND GRAINS

Wheat is still probably the most widely grown grain. The U.S., Canada, and Russia are the major producers, although it is also grown throughout Western Europe. China, India, Argentina, Australia, and Pakistan are other wheat-growing areas. More than ninety percent of wheat is grown in the Northern Hemisphere. Wheat is either hard or soft, the soft being used for general purpose flours, containing less gluten and protein than the hard. Hard wheat is better for bread flours and for the production of pasta.

Wheat has always been the main crop for the production of **flour** for breadmaking. It contains more gluten – the substance which creates the framework of bread and makes the dough elastic – than other flours and consequently produces a lighter, more palatable loaf. Whole-wheat flour, as the name suggests, is milled from the whole grain so contains all the nutrients.

Bulgur is a form of cracked wheat made by boiling and then baking whole grains of wheat, which are then cracked. This technique was probably developed as a method of storage, and bulgur is particularly common in the Middle East. It is most often used in salads such as

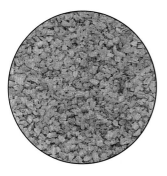

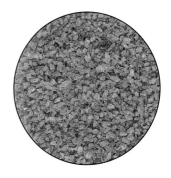

CRACKED WHEAT GRANOLA BULGUR

tabbouleh, but I also like cooking with it – it makes excellent risotto-style dishes and cooks in approximately the same time as rice.

Wheat flakes are used mainly as a breakfast cereal. **Wheat germ** is the heart of the grain and is generally added to breakfast cereals as a highly nutritious dietary supplement. **Wheat bran** is the most common form of bran and is the by-product of milling white flour. It is rich in fiber and is added to breads or sold to be added to cereals to boost fiber in them.

Semolina and **couscous** are both wheat products. Semolina is a meal ground from durum wheat, a particularly hard form of wheat used in pasta-making. Semolina is used in milk puddings and readily absorbs liquid. I scatter it lightly under fish or meat that is to be cooked wrapped in pastry – the semolina absorbs any juices and prevents the pastry from becoming soggy during cooking. Couscous, pellets of processed fine and coarse semolinas mixed together then sifted into shape, gives its name to a dish when it is steamed over a stew with which it is served.

Barley is available as a whole grain, which is known as **pot barley**, to be used in stews. It may take up to three hours to cook and never really becomes soft and tender. **Pearl barley** is the husked, polished berry and is traditionally used in soups, both for flavor and as a thickener.

Barley flour is used in many eastern European countries to make bread, but it gives a rather gray loaf with a dense texture, and is considerably less palatable than a wheat loaf. It has a sweet flavor, however, and is a useful ingredient in a mixed-grain loaf when combined with wheat and rye flours. Barley may also be used to make a form of oatmeal, but is most commonly associated with the brewing industry, where it is used in the production of malt for both beers and whiskey.

Rye is widely grown and used in northern European and Scandinavian countries, being tolerant of cold weather and acid soils. Until the nineteenth century, **rye flour** was more commonly used in some areas for bread than wheat, but as soon as white bread became fashionable, so did wheat flour. Rye flour is used to make "black" breads and crackers. It does not have the same gluten content as wheat so the resulting yeasted breads are heavier and do not rise as much. **Crackers** were originally made to prolong the storage life of the rye crop. Short summers in northern Europe meant that the rye often had to be harvested before it was really ripe, and the unripe grain did not store well, being too full of moisture. Roughly ground and baked into slabs, it was found that these fiber-rich crackers kept well and could be stored right through the long winter months. Some rye is

ABOVE CREAMED CORN CORNBREAD (SEE PAGE 194)

grown in North America and it is often fermented to make rye whiskey. Rye is darker in color than wheat and has a stronger flavor, although it is sometimes processed into a white flour which then loses most of the distinctive rye flavor.

Somehow **oats** have a far more rustic image than the other grains and cereal crops. They are a hardy crop, and are often made into a gruel or mush. Oats are a soft grain and are therefore not suitable for milling into flour. The crop is adaptable and is thought to have been grown in ancient Mesopotamia and Abyssinia, both of which had very warm climates. It would have provided useful cover for more tender plants, shielding them from the sun. Oats are now usually grown in colder climates in the Northern Hemisphere, in the U.S. and Canada, Europe, and Russia.

Oats are a good source of iron, potassium, and vitamin B, as well as being rich in fiber and carbohydrates, with some protein and fat. **Oat flakes**, or **rolled oats**, are used for baking and for oatmeal, a warming breakfast dish (especially good with brown sugar on very cold days!). **Oatmeal** or **Irish oatmeal** is milled in various grades and may be used for baking, especially oatcakes, and features in the Scottish national dish, haggis. **Oat bran** is the fiber-rich outer casing of the oats. It can be added to most breakfast cereals or mixed with rolled oats for hot oatmeal.

Millet is thought of by many people as little more than bird food, yet it is widely grown and consumed in Africa and in some countries in Asia and Europe. It makes excellent savory baked goods – it has a creamy texture and must be boiled before being turned into a finished dish – I have used it for rissoles (sweet- or savory-filled turnovers) and in baking. It may also be used as a thickener, especially for soups and stews, in which case it should be cooked in the cooking liquid of the dish. It does swell considerably, so don't be tempted to add too much to the dish.

Corn or **maize** is the biggest crop in North America, which grows over forty percent of the world's total production. It grows very high – I have worked in corn fields in southern England where the crop has been taller than I am. The terms corn and maize are interchangeable; therefore, cornstarch and maize flour are the same basic product, although they may vary in color. Corn, when on the cob, is very high in dietary fiber.

Corn is available processed as **cornstarch**, a very fine flour used for thickening liquids for sauces, stews, and soups. It is generally white. **Cornmeal** and **polenta** are not quite so finely ground and are usually yellow in color. Polenta is produced in Italy and is generally made into a solid, oatmeal-like substance which is delicious sliced or baked and served with soups or stews. Corn or maize flour is used extensively throughout the U.S. for bread and gives a much sweeter flavor than wheat flour.

Hominy and **grits** are common foods in the American South. The first is the dried corn kernels, also widely available ready-to-eat in cans. When dry, hominy should be soaked to reconstitute and then baked or fried, although I prefer to use it in casseroles, especially those made with pork. Even when left to soak

overnight, hominy may take up to five hours of simmering to soften. Grits are ground hominy and have a semolina-like texture. They cook much more quickly than the whole kernels and are often served with bacon and eggs.

Blue cornmeal is highly valued because of its unusual appearance. The flour is usually made into tortilla chips or sold for making pancakes. It really is blue and comes from a dark blue strain of corn. Apart from culinary uses, it may be found in some cosmetic products, such as face scrubs and deep cleansers.

Popcorn is a particularly hard corn kernel which turns itself inside out when cooked in a popcorn-maker or a dry, covered pan. The pan should be well sealed, otherwise the exploding corn may cover your kitchen. The beneficial fiber content of popcorn is usually more than canceled out by the amount of butter or salt used to coat it.

One of the more unusual grains available is **buckwheat**, which is really the fruit or seed of a plant closely related to rhubarb and sorrel, and therefore not really a grain at all. It does, however, cook like a grain. It is available both raw and roasted, the latter having a deeper and slightly more palatable flavor. It is rich in vitamins A and B and calcium, as well as carbohydrates. Buckwheat is available as groats (grains) or as flour. The flour, which is an unusual gray color, is used for pancakes, crêpes, and muffins; generally, I find bread made with buckwheat very unappealing and not to my taste. The most common use for buckwheat flour is in the making of pancakes and blinis – little yeasted pancakes most commonly from Russia, which are served with sour cream, caviar, and smoked salmon.

Rice is the staple food of about half the population of the world and is grown on every continent except Antarctica. It is a cereal grass and while it is grown on tropical hillsides, it is widely grown in water on marshy flooded land, usually known as paddy-fields, in conditions in which other grains – such as barley and wheat – would not survive.

Rice is native to India and Indo-China but its cultivation quickly spread throughout the East. Ancient Chinese records speak of planting ceremonies after permission to grow rice had been granted by the emperor. The term "paddy-field" actually comes from the Malay word *padi* for unhusked rice grains.

The Romans brought rice back to Italy following their travels to the East and grew it in the flooded plains of the Po Valley. Arborio rice, used to make risotto, is grown there to this day. As the Roman Empire expanded, so too did the cultivation of rice, moving to Spain and parts of Africa. Today, there is also a great deal of rice grown in the U.S., but this really came about by accident when a spice ship from Madagascar, bound for England, was blown off course, and ended up in Charleston, South Carolina. In gratitude to his hosts for their hospitality, the captain of the ship presented them with some of his cargo of rough seed rice, which has flourished in the south ever since.

THE NUTRITIVE VALUE OF RICE

Rice is not fattening; like pasta, it's the food you serve with it that can do the damage! All rices are valuable sources of B-group vitamins and minerals, especially potassium and phosphorus. Brown rice contains both more fiber and more protein than white rice and is also a good source of calcium and iron.

Brown rice is simply the unmilled or unpolished grain, so all varieties of rice should be available as brown rice. It is quite easy to find brown long grain, short grain, and basmati rices, and brown arborio rice is sometimes available in good health shops. Brown rice takes longer to cook than white; never add salt to the water during cooking because this can toughen the grain. The cooking time may be slightly shortened by soaking the rice in the measured amount of water before cooking.

Instant or **converted rice** is partially steamed before the milling process. This forces the nutrients from the bran into the rice grain so that they are retained during milling. Instant brown rice is now widely available.

There are many other types of rice, most of which are most commonly available in their white or polished forms. Among my favorites are **arborio** and **carnarolli** rice, both used to make **risotto**, and **basmati**, the finest grain of all the rices, which is grown in the foothills of the Himalayas. **Camargue red rice** is an unpolished rice grown in very small quantities in southern France, which has a very nutty flavor as well as a very distinctive color.

Wild rice is actually the seed from an aquatic grass grown in the northern U.S. and in Canada. It has very long, slender, almost-black grains. Originally very expensive, being hand-harvested from a boat, wild rice is now grown commercially, although the cultivated grains do not have quite the same flavor as the truly wild variety. Wild rice has a far higher nutritive value than either of the two main cereal crops, regular rice and wheat. Its protein contains all nine of

the essential amino acids, making it a complete protein. Because it is unpolished, it is also very rich in fiber.

Rice bran is the husk of the rice, removed during milling. It is not a common product except in countries where rice is processed, but it is used as a supplement to breakfast cereals. **Flaked rice** cooks quickly and is used mainly in puddings, although it is often added to granolas. **Rice flour** is used especially in Chinese cookery to make rice noodles, but can also be used to thicken sauces and in cakes and pastries for people who are allergic to wheat flour. It is very fine and is often used in the cosmetics industry as a base for makeup. **Ground rice** is the rice equivalent of semolina, fine and grainy and used for puddings and cookies.

Beans: dried foods rich in nutrients

Beans and legumes are not only a good source of fiber in the diet – red kidney beans, for example, contain 4.5 percent fiber and as much protein as meat (24 percent), and much the same is true of chickpeas and lentils – all beans also contain vitamins, especially B-group, and minerals, notably iron. There is a wide variety of beans in different shapes and colors, making them an invaluable part of our diet. From the eating angle most of them taste remarkably similar, however, chickpeas and adzuki beans are in my opinion outstanding in their flavor. After that, the choice is governed by appearance, the dish for which they are intended, and the length of cooking time available.

For the recipes in this book, I have used my favorite beans, the ones that I generally have in my cupboard. I have not included any recipes for soy beans, for example, as I do not keep them at home. They could, however, be used in any of the recipes calling for a similar size of bean; for example, navy beans or black-eyed peas.

Adzuki, or azuki beans are common in Chinese and Japanese cooking and grow in both countries. They are a rich, nutty brown in color and very small. The most obvious feature of the beans is their slightly sweet flavor – they are often used in sweet dishes – and I have included them in both a savory casserole and a delicious sweet dessert cobbler.

Mung beans are a similar size to adzuki beans but are green in color. They may be sprouted for a salad vegetable, and are sometimes ground into flour. They are most commonly used in Chinese and Indian cookery, but I have used them in a recipe for vegetable turnovers.

Lentils are unique among beans, because they require no soaking before they are cooked; this makes them an instant food. Red lentils are often dropped in food parcels to disaster areas because they can be cooked up into a paste or dal immediately, providing protein and other valuable nutrients. Lentils are red, yellow, green, or brown. I use mainly red and green lentils, and you will find both in recipes in this book – the lentil soufflé is delicious and most unusual.

There are a number of medium-sized white beans that are suitable for general cookery. **Haricots** can be used in a variety of recipes and keep their shape when cooked in casseroles, the most famous of which is the French cassoulet.

Navy beans were the original baked bean and are widely used in North America. **Cannellini beans** are Italian white kidney beans, slightly more elongated than navy beans, and are often used with tuna fish to make a classic Italian antipasto, although I have used **flageolets** (comparable to baby lima beans) for my tuna bean salad. These are also a member of the kidney bean family, but have an attractive green color. They are generally available dried and canned, rarely fresh, and are a very good cupboard standby.

Chickpeas (garbanzos), called *chana* in India, are large, pea-shaped beans that are used extensively in Mediterranean, Indian, and Middle Eastern cookery. They have a distinctive nutty flavor and are used in casseroles and in dips, the most famous of which is hummus. Chickpeas are a natural partner to sesame seeds and are often used with tahini, a delicious Middle Eastern paste of toasted ground sesame seeds.

ABOVE CHICKEN AND BEAN RISOTTO (SEE PAGE 134)

Other medium-sized beans include **black kidney beans**, used in South American cookery (these are different from the small, round black soy beans, fermented and used in Japanese cookery), and **pinto beans**, which are brown in color and are the traditional beans used in Mexican dishes, including chili con carne. They also have the distinction of cooking more quickly than most other beans. Reddish-brown **pink beans** are also used in chili, particularly in the southern states. **Great Northern beans** are large white beans resembling lima beans in shape but having a more delicate flavor. They grow in the U.S. midwest and are popular for baked bean dishes. The smaller white **navy beans**, so named because the U.S. Navy has served them since the 1800s, are widely used in soups and baked beans. **Red kidney beans** are the meat of the kidney bean family: large beans that are widely used because of their color and flavor. Kidney beans should always be boiled vigorously for the first ten minutes of their cooking time, in order to destroy any toxins that may be in the beans.

Fava beans, known in Europe as **broad beans**, are large and meaty in texture. **Lima beans**, also called **butter beans**, are usually large and white in color, and have a sweet, creamy flavor, good for soups and casseroles.

There are two other beans that are less common but worth mentioning. **Ful medames** are an Egyptian bean, and a casserole of these beans is to Egypt what roast beef and Yorkshire pudding are to England: a national dish. **Gunga peas**, also known as **pigeon peas** are similar in size to black-eyed peas or beans, and have a rich earthy flavor. They are widely used throughout the Caribbean and southern U.S. and are especially favored for any dish where they are accompanied by rice and a flavorsome sauce.

Beans and lentils

All dried beans should be soaked before use. Cover with cold water and leave overnight. Make sure you allow soaking time before you prepare a dish containing dried beans. Lentils do not require soaking.

MUNG BEANS

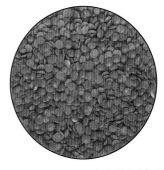

EGYPTIAN LENTILS

CHICKPEAS

BLACK BEANS

KIDNEY BEANS

GREEN LENTILS

HARICOT BEANS

CANNELINI BEANS

BORLOTTI BEANS

ADZUKI BEANS

FAVA BEANS

Other fiber-rich foods to include in your diet

Dried fruits provide a rich and delicious source of fiber and are excellent for high-fiber desserts.

Pasta is a derivative of wheat and is also a high-fiber food. Whole-wheat pasta contains more fiber than others and is becoming widely available in stores.

Nuts are a valuable source of dietary fiber and should always be included in a mixed diet. They are, however, very high in fat, so care should be taken to eat them only in moderation. They typically contain 2 percent fiber, and 59 percent fat, so be warned!

Changing to a high-fiber diet

High-fiber eating makes sense when you consider the benefits of eating food in as natural a state as possible. Of course, not every food that you eat has to be high-fiber — you may chose to keep to white pasta but change to whole-wheat bread and start eating more fresh fruits, salads, and vegetables. As with any eating regime, it is a good idea to eat a wide variety of foods and enjoy them — do not rely just on sprinkling handfuls of bran over everything to increase your fiber intake. This will not be good for your taste buds or for your digestion.

Using the recipes in this book

I have included a wide variety of recipes in this book but, even so, they are really only an introduction to the huge selection of dishes that can be made within the bounds of a high-fiber diet. When you feel confident with a recipe or ingredient, try experimenting for yourself.

Most of the recipes are simple and straightforward. However, high-fiber baking includes more bran and moisture-hungry foods than regular baking, so it is advisable to make batters a degree or so wetter than otherwise.

I like to use butter and olive oil in my kitchen at home. In most of these recipes, sunflower margarine can replace the butter, but always use it straight from the refrigerator. You may use your own choice of fat or oil, but always consider the flavor of the finished dish.

A good diet should not only be high in fiber but also low in fat and sugars. Cakes and cookies should be regarded as treats and not everyday foods, and the amount of extra fat added to foods should be kept to a minimum.

Some of these dishes may be very different from the foods you have been used to eating for many years. I hope you will enjoy trying them, and that you will discover a whole new culinary repertoire that will not only be good for your health, but tempt your tastebuds as well.

1 Soups and chowders

A high-fiber soup can easily be a filling meal in itself, so take care when menu planning, especially for a three- or four-course meal. Many of these soups and chowders are made with root vegetables or beans which give a thick texture, especially if the soup is puréed at the end of cooking. Thin the soup if you wish by adding extra stock or milk, but remember that soups are essentially comfort food and many people prefer them thick.

Soups should always be served piping hot or chilled; a tepid soup is a disaster. Do not boil soups that have had light cream or fruit juices, such as orange or lemon, added to them – the cream may curdle and the flavor of the fruit will become tainted. Chilled soups are always better served over crushed ice.

The secret of any successful soup is the flavor of the stock used in its making. Stocks are not difficult to prepare and consist of bones and vegetable peelings, a few herbs, and some peppercorns. I collect all my onion skins, carrot scrapings, and other clean vegetable waste and place them in a large stockpot with plenty of water, herbs, and a light seasoning of salt. Bring to a boil then simmer very slowly for two to three hours, until a rich, dark liquor is produced. Strain the stock then season lightly, to taste. The stock may be reduced to intensify the flavor, in which case it should not be seasoned until it has been boiled. Never cover the pot or the resulting stock may be musty in flavor and cloudy; the stock should be simmered very slowly, with just an occasional bubble breaking the surface.

LEFT SMOKED FISH CHOWDER (SEE PAGE 50)

orange and butternut soup

I FIRST TASTED THIS SOUP ON HOLIDAY IN SOUTH AFRICA. BE CAREFUL NOT TO BOIL THE SOUP AFTER ADDING THE ORANGE JUICE OR THE FLAVOR WILL BECOME TAINTED. **SERVES 4 TO 6**

1 large onion, chopped

2 Tbsp (25 mL) vegetable oil

1 to 2 butternut squashes, weighing about 2 lb (900 g), peeled and diced

Grated rind and juice of 2 oranges

6 cups (1.5 L) rich vegetable stock

2 bay leaves

Salt and freshly ground black pepper

Nutmeg

2 Tbsp (25 mL) chopped fresh parsley

1 Cook the onion in the oil until softened but not browned, then add the prepared squash and cook slowly for 5 minutes, stirring occasionally. Stir in grated orange, then add the stock, bay leaves, and seasonings. Bring the soup to a boil, then cover and simmer for 40 minutes, until the squash is tender and cooked through.

2 Allow the soup to cool slightly, remove the bay leaves, then purée in a blender or food processor until smooth. Rinse the pot and return the soup to it, adding the orange juice. Reheat the soup slowly - do not let it boil - then season to taste. Add the chopped parsley and sprinkle with nutmeg just before serving.

sausage, apple and pasta soup

USE CUBED CHEESE INSTEAD OF THE SAUSAGES, AND LET IT MELT INTO THE SOUP. **SERVES 4**

- **2 Tbsp (25 mL) vegetable oil**
- **1 lb (450 g) pork sausages**
- **1 medium onion, finely chopped**
- **1 medium red bell pepper, seeded and chopped**
- **2 cups (500 mL) dry cider**
- **4 cups (1 L) vegetable stock**
- **Salt and freshly ground black pepper**
- **½ tsp (2 mL) nutmeg**
- **1 cup (250 mL) whole-wheat macaroni**
- **1 large Granny Smith apple, cored, peeled, and finely chopped**
- **½ cup (125 mL) grated Cheddar cheese (optional)**

1 Heat the oil in a large pot, then add the sausages and cook quickly until browned on all sides. Add the onion and pepper and cook more slowly for 3 to 4 minutes, until they are tender.

2 Add the cider and stock to the pan with the seasonings and bring to a boil. Simmer the soup for 30 minutes, then remove the sausages with a slotted spoon. Add the macaroni and simmer for a further 10 to 12 minutes, or until the pasta is just cooked. Slice the sausages while the macaroni is cooking, then return the meat to the pot. Add the apple just before the pasta is cooked – do not simmer it for more than 2 minutes.

3 Season the soup to taste then serve immediately, with or without grated cheese.

artichoke and corn soup

SWEET AND CREAMY, THIS IS A REAL WINTER WARMER. **SERVES 6**

- **1 onion, finely chopped**
- **2 Tbsp (25 mL) butter**
- **1 lb (450 g) Jerusalem artichokes, washed and roughly chopped**
- **2 cups (250 g) frozen corn**
- **3 cups (750 mL) rich vegetable stock**
- **Salt and freshly ground black pepper**
- **2 tsp (2 mL) dried red pepper flakes (optional)**
- **1⅓ cups (300 mL) milk**
- **3 Tbsp (40 mL) sour cream**
- **Freshly chopped chives for garnish**

1 Cook the onion in the butter until soft, then add the artichokes and corn. Stir the vegetables over the heat until the corn starts to defrost, then add the stock and seasonings and bring to a boil. Simmer for 35 to 40 minutes, until the artichokes are tender.

2 Cool the soup slightly, then purée until smooth in a blender or food processor. Rinse the pot and return the soup to it with the milk. Reheat gently, seasoning to taste, then stir in the sour cream and garnish with chopped chives just before serving.

parsnip and apple soup

THE TART APPLE GIVES A REAL PUNCH TO THIS NEW CLASSIC CURRIED PARSNIP SOUP. **SERVES 4 TO 6**

1 large onion, chopped

1 Tbsp (15 mL) sunflower oil

1 tsp (5 mL) mild curry powder

1 lb (450 g) parsnips, chopped

1 medium Granny Smith apple, peeled, cored, and sliced

5 cups (1.25 L) rich vegetable stock

Salt and freshly ground black pepper

Juice of ½ lemon

Chopped fresh parsley or cilantro to garnish

1 Cook the onion in the oil for 4 to 5 minutes until soft, then stir in the curry powder with the parsnips. Cook for a further 2 to 3 minutes before adding the apple and stock. Bring to a boil, then simmer for 30 minutes or until the parsnip is tender.

2 Allow the soup to cool slightly, then purée until smooth in a blender or food processor. Rinse the pot and return the soup to it, adding sufficient water to thin the soup if necessary. Reheat gently, then season to taste with salt and pepper. Add the lemon juice just before serving and garnish with parsley or cilantro.

french onion soup

THE TRADITIONAL PICK-ME-UP FOR THE EARLY MORNING AFTER THE NIGHT BEFORE. **SERVES 6**

2 cups (500 mL) sliced onions

1 Tbsp (15 mL) butter

2 Tbsp (25 mL) olive oil

2 Tbsp (25 mL) whole-wheat flour

4 cups (1 L) rich vegetable stock

Salt and freshly ground black pepper

3 bay leaves

4 to 6 slices quality whole-wheat French bread

½ cup (125 mL) grated Swiss cheese

1 Cook the onions in the butter and oil over high heat in a large pot until softened and well browned; this may take up to 10 minutes. Stir the flour into the onions and cook gently for 1 to 2 minutes. Remove from heat and gradually add the stock to the pot, stirring all the time, then season lightly and add the bay leaves. Return the pot to the heat and bring the soup gradually to a boil, cover and simmer for 45 minutes. The soup should be a rich, dark brown color.

2 Preheat the broiler. Remove the bay leaves and season the soup to taste. Fill 6 individual flameproof serving bowls ⅔ full with soup. Drop a slice of bread into each bowl, then scatter the cheese over the bread. Cook under the hot broiler until the cheese has melted and is bubbling. Serve immediately, with a slice of bread in each portion.

31

lima bean and parsnip chowder

USE SQUASH INSTEAD OF PARSNIP IF YOU PREFER. **SERVES 6**

1 large onion, chopped

2 Tbsp (25 mL) oil

1 medium clove garlic

1½ cups (375 mL) diced parsnip

1 cup (250 mL) lima beans, soaked overnight

4½ cups (1.1 L) rich vegetable stock

Salt and freshly ground black pepper

Nutmeg

1 cup (250 mL) milk

2 slices good quality whole-wheat bread

2 Tbsp (25 mL) butter or margarine

1 Tbsp (15 mL) chopped fresh parsley

1 Cook the onion in the oil until soft, then add the garlic and parsnip and continue cooking until the parsnip starts to brown. Drain the soaked lima beans and rinse them thoroughly under running water. Add the beans to the pot with the stock, some salt, pepper, and nutmeg. Bring the soup to a boil, then cover and simmer slowly for about an hour, until the beans are tender.

2 Allow the soup to cool slightly, then purée it until smooth in a blender or food processor. Rinse the pot and return the soup to it with the milk. Heat gently while preparing the croutons, but do not allow the soup to boil.

3 Toast the bread on one side only. Beat the butter or margarine with a little salt and pepper and the chopped parsley. Spread the mixture over the untoasted side of the bread and cook until lightly browned. Trim away the crusts if you wish, then cut the bread into tiny triangles or squares. Season the soup to taste, and serve with the croutons.

cream of cauliflower and cumin soup

I LOVE THE SUBTLY SPICED FLAVOR OF THE CAULIFLOWER THAT DOMINATES THIS SOUP. **SERVES 6**

1 tsp (5 mL) cumin seeds

⅔ cup (175 mL) diced onion

1 Tbsp (15 mL) oil

5 cups (1.25 L) roughly chopped cauliflower, florets and stalks

2 cups (500 mL) milk

3 cups (750 mL) rich vegetable stock

Salt and freshly ground black pepper

1 Heat a dry skillet until hot, then add the cumin seeds and roast for 1 to 2 minutes. Cool slightly, then grind to a fine powder in a pestle and mortar or with the end of a rolling pin.

2 Cook the onion slowly in the oil until soft but not browned, then add the ground cumin and cauliflower. Continue cooking slowly for 1 to 2 minutes, then add the milk, stock, and seasonings. Bring to a boil, then simmer for just 10 minutes. Cool slightly before blending in a blender or food processor until smooth. Rinse the pot, return the soup to it and reheat, seasoning to taste.

minted pea soup

YOUNG PEAS AND FRESH MINT ARE ESSENTIAL, BUT YOU CAN SERVE THE SOUP HOT OR CHILLED OVER CRUSHED ICE, AS YOU PREFER. **SERVES 6**

1 small onion, finely chopped

2 Tbsp (25 mL) butter

1 lb (450 g) peas, frozen or, preferably, fresh

2 Tbsp (25 mL) chopped fresh mint

5 cups (1.25 L) water

Grated rind of 1 lime

Salt and white pepper to taste

Light cream

1 Cook the onion slowly in the butter until soft but not brown; it is important to soften the onion really well as this soup has a very short cooking time. Stir in the peas and the mint, then add the water and bring the soup to a boil. Simmer for only 3 to 4 minutes, until the peas are just cooked – this will preserve the bright color of the soup.

2 Cool the soup slightly, then add the lime rind and purée until smooth in a blender or food processor. Rinse the pot and return the soup to it, seasoning to taste with salt and white pepper. Reheat gently or allow to cool completely before chilling. Serve with a swirl of light cream.

34 **ABOVE** BROCCOLI SOUP

pumpkin and carrot soup

IF LOVAGE IS NOT AVAILABLE, USE CELERY OR FLAT-LEAVED PARSLEY AND OREGANO. **SERVES 8 TO 10**

1 large onion, finely chopped

1 Tbsp (15 mL) vegetable oil

1 lb (450 g) carrots, sliced

1 lb (450 g) pumpkin purée, fresh or canned

6 cups (1.5 L) rich vegetable stock

Salt and freshly ground black pepper

2 Tbsp (25 mL) freshly chopped lovage

2 cups (500 mL) milk

1 Tbsp (15 mL) butter or margarine

1 large clove garlic, crushed

2 slices whole-wheat bread, toasted

1 Cook the onion in the oil until lightly browned, then add the carrots and cook gently until just softening. Stir in the pumpkin purée, then add the stock and bring to a boil, adding the seasonings and half the lovage. Cover and simmer slowly for 30 to 40 minutes, until the carrots are tender.

2 Allow the soup to cool slightly, then purée until smooth in a blender or food processor. Rinse the pot and return the soup to it with the milk, reheating gently and adding extra seasoning, if required, to taste.

3 Beat the butter and add the remaining lovage and the garlic, then season lightly. Toast the bread, spread it lightly with the butter and cut into small squares or triangles. Drop the toasts into the soup just before serving.

broccoli soup

I PREFER TO USE WATER RATHER THAN STOCK TO ALLOW THE DELICATE BROCCOLI FLAVOR THROUGH. **SERVES 6**

1 large onion, finely chopped

1 Tbsp (15 mL) butter

2 large heads broccoli, weighing about 1 lb (450 g) in total

Salt and freshly ground black pepper

4 cups (1 L) water

2 cups (500 mL) milk

Nutmeg, to taste

Light cream (optional)

1 Cook the onion in the butter until softened but not browned. Trim the broccoli and chop it, using the stalks and the florets. Add the broccoli to the pot, tossing it in the hot juices, then season lightly and add the water. Bring to a boil then simmer for 30 to 40 minutes, until the broccoli is tender.

2 Cool slightly, then purée the soup in a blender or food processor. Rinse the pot and return the soup to it with the milk; heat slowly until almost at a boil. Remove from the heat. Season to taste with salt, pepper, and nutmeg and serve immediately with a swirl of cream.

chestnut and blue cheese soup

A RICH, SMOKY, AND DELICIOUS SOUP. I USE FROZEN CHESTNUTS FOR CONVENIENCE, BUT FRESH OR CANNED WORK JUST AS WELL. **SERVES 6**

- **1 Tbsp (15 mL) vegetable oil**
- **6 to 8 scallions, trimmed and finely chopped**
- **4 strips bacon, chopped**
- **1 lb (450 g) peeled chestnuts, fresh, frozen, or canned; or 2 cups (500 mL) dried chestnuts, soaked overnight**
- **4 cups (1 L) vegetable stock**
- **2 bay leaves**
- **Salt and freshly ground black pepper**
- **2 cups (500 mL) milk**
- **¾ cup (175 mL) crumbled blue cheese, e.g. Danish or Stilton**
- **Chopped fresh chives to garnish**

1 Heat the oil in a pot, add the scallions and bacon and cook slowly until the scallions are soft. Add the chestnuts, stock, and bay leaves with a little salt and pepper. Bring the soup to a boil, cover and simmer for 30 minutes.

2 Remove the bay leaf, allow the soup to cool slightly and purée until smooth in a blender or food processor. Rinse the pot and return the soup to it, then add the milk and return gradually to a boil. Season the soup to taste, then add the crumbled cheese just before serving. Garnish with chopped chives.

tomato, orange and lentil soup

THE ADVANTAGE OF USING LENTILS OVER OTHER BEANS OR LEGUMES IS THAT THEY DON'T REQUIRE SOAKING BEFORE USING. **SERVES 4 TO 6**

- **1 large onion, finely chopped**
- **1 Tbsp (15 mL) vegetable oil**
- **Grated rind and juice of 1 large orange**
- **½ cup (125 mL) red lentils**
- **14-fl oz (398-mL) can chopped tomatoes**
- **4 cups (1 L) rich vegetable stock**
- **Salt and freshly ground black pepper**
- **A few small basil leaves**

1 Cook the onion in the oil until soft then add the orange rind and lentils. Quickly stir in the chopped tomatoes, add the stock and a little seasoning. Bring the soup to a boil and simmer for 30 minutes, until the lentils are soft.

2 Allow the soup to cool slightly, add half the basil, then purée until smooth in a blender or food processor. Rinse the pot and return the soup to it, adding the orange juice and the remaining basil leaves, torn into small pieces. Heat the soup gently – do not allow it to boil after adding the orange juice or the flavor will be tainted. Season to taste and serve with crusty bread.

beet soup with horseradish

A LIGHTER VARIATION ON CLASSIC RUSSIAN BORSCHT, THIS PEPPERY
SOUP IS DELICIOUS – BUT TAKE CARE THAT YOUR BEETS HAVE NOT
BEEN DRESSED IN VINEGAR BEFORE USE OR YOUR SOUP WILL TASTE
FOUL! FRESH BEETS ARE BEST. **SERVES 6**

1 large onion, finely chopped

2 medium white turnips, diced

1 Tbsp (15 mL) vegetable oil

1 lb (450 g) cooked beets, diced

6 cups (1.5 L) rich vegetable or beef stock

Salt and freshly ground black pepper

4 bay leaves

2 tsp (25 mL) grated horseradish

1 Tbsp (15 mL) freshly chopped chives

½ cup (125 mL) sour cream

1 Cook the onion and the turnip in the oil until softened but not
browned, then add the beet and the stock and bring to a boil.
Reduce the heat, add the seasonings, bay leaves, and 1 tsp (5 mL)
horseradish, cover and simmer for 30 to 40 minutes.

2 Allow the soup to cool slightly and remove the bay leaves.
Then purée until smooth in a blender or food processor. Rinse
the pot and return the soup to it and reheat the soup gently. Mix
the remaining horseradish and the chives into the sour cream.
Season the soup to taste and serve with a large dollop of the flavored
sour cream in each portion and top with chives.

fennel and walnut soup

THIS ANISEED-FLAVORED SOUP IS A DINNER PARTY FAVORITE. **SERVES 4 TO 6**

- **1 large onion, finely chopped**
- **1 large bulb fennel, trimmed and sliced**
- **3 sticks celery, trimmed and sliced**
- **2 Tbsp (25 mL) vegetable oil**
- **1 plump garlic clove, finely sliced**
- **2 bay leaves**
- **5½ cups (1.4 L) vegetable stock**
- **Salt and freshly ground black pepper**
- **½ cup (125 mL) sour cream or plain yogurt**
- **½ cup (125 mL) walnuts, finely chopped**
- **Chopped fresh parsley mixed with fennel fronds and celery leaves to garnish**

1 Cook the prepared vegetables slowly in the oil until soft but not browned. Add the garlic, bay leaves, and stock and bring the soup to a boil. Cover the pot and simmer for 30 to 40 minutes, until the vegetables are tender.

2 Cool the soup slightly and remove bay leaves. Purée until smooth in a blender or food processor. Rinse the pot and return the soup to it. Reheat gently and season to taste with salt and pepper, then stir in the sour cream or yogurt. Add the walnuts just before serving and garnish with any reserved chopped fennel fronds, the celery leaves, and parsley.

spinach and zucchini soup

THIS SOUP HAS A STRONG, WARMING PEPPERY FLAVOR. **SERVES 8**

- **1 small onion, finely chopped**
- **1 Tbsp (15 mL) oil**
- **1 to 2 cloves garlic, crushed**
- **1 lb (450 g) freshly, washed or frozen spinach**
- **2 medium zucchini, trimmed and grated**
- **6 cups (1.5 L) rich vegetable stock**
- **Salt and freshly ground black pepper**
- **Nutmeg, to taste**
- **1 Tbsp (15 mL) fresh basil leaves, roughly torn**
- **Grated zucchini and whole-wheat croutons to garnish**

1 Cook the onion in the oil until soft then add the garlic, spinach, and zucchini. Mix well, then stir in the stock and bring the soup to a boil. Season lightly with salt, pepper, and nutmeg and simmer for 20 minutes.

2 Allow the soup to cool slightly, add the basil leaves and purée until smooth in a blender or food processor. Rinse the pot and return the soup to it. Reheat gently, adding extra seasoning to taste and serve the soup garnished with raw grated zucchini and whole-wheat croutons.

mexican bean soup

PINTO BEANS ARE TRADITIONAL, BUT IF YOU CAN'T GET THEM, USE EXTRA
KIDNEY BEANS INSTEAD. **SERVES 6**

½ cup (125 mL) red kidney beans,
    soaked overnight

½ cup (125 mL) pinto beans, soaked
    overnight

1 large onion, finely chopped

1 Tbsp (15 mL) oil

1 red chile, seeded and finely
    chopped

1 large clove garlic, finely sliced

1 tsp (5 mL) mild chili powder

1 Tbsp (15 mL) cilantro leaves

6 cups (1.5 L) rich vegetable stock

1 Tbsp (15 mL) tomato purée

Salt and freshly ground black pepper

½ cup (125 mL) Cheddar cheese, grated

Guacamole for serving, see page 95

1 Drain the beans and rinse them thoroughly under cold running water; set aside until needed. Cook the onion in the oil until soft, add the chile, garlic, and chili powder and cook for another minute.

2 Stir the beans into the pot, then add the cilantro, stock, tomato purée, and seasonings. Bring the soup to a boil and cook for 10 minutes, then simmer slowly for 45 to 60 minutes, until the beans are soft. Allow the soup to cool and purée until smooth in a blender or food processor. Rinse the pan then return the soup to it and reheat gently, seasoning to taste with salt and pepper. Scatter the cheese over the soup just before serving and set out a dish of guacamole.

armenian soup

THIS SPICY LENTIL SOUP IS SWEETENED AND THICKENED WITH APRICOTS AND GOLDEN RAISINS. **SERVES 6**

1 large onion, finely chopped

2 Tbsp (25 mL) olive oil

1 tsp (15 mL) ground ginger

1 tsp (15 mL) ground cumin

½ tsp (2 mL) ground cinnamon

2 medium tomatoes, diced

1 cup (250 mL) red lentils

6 cups (1.5 L) rich vegetable stock

Salt and freshly ground black pepper

½ cup (125 mL) ready-to-eat dried
    apricots, roughly chopped

⅓ cup (90 mL) golden raisins

Sour cream or plain yogurt (optional)

1 Cook the onion in the oil in a large pot until soft, add the spices and cook for 1 minute over low heat. Add the tomatoes and lentils, stir in the stock and slowly bring the soup to a boil. Season well, add the dried fruit, cover, and simmer for 30 minutes, until the lentils and vegetables are soft.

2 Season the soup to taste. It may be puréed if preferred, then thinned down with a little extra stock or water. Serve with a dollop of sour cream or yogurt.

gazpacho

THIS IS THE CLASSIC COLD TOMATO SOUP OF SPAIN – AND THE TRICK
IS TO CHILL IT REALLY WELL. **SERVES 8**

½ cucumber, chopped

1 medium green bell pepper, seeded and finely chopped

1 medium red onion, finely chopped

3 medium cloves garlic, crushed

⅔ cup (150 mL) fresh white bread crumbs

Three 14-fl oz (398-mL) cans chopped tomatoes

Salt

¼ cup (60 mL) white wine vinegar

¼ cup (60 mL) fruity olive oil

1 cup (250 mL) water or vegetable stock

Sugar

GARNISH

1 small green bell pepper, seeded and finely chopped

½ cucumber, seeded and finely chopped

1 small red onion, finely chopped

Crushed ice if available

1 Purée all the soup ingredients together in a blender or food
processor, adding as much water or stock as necessary to make a
thick, smooth creamy soup. Season well, adding sugar to taste, then
chill the soup with about 12 ice cubes until very cold. The soup
will become slightly more liquid as the ice melts in it.

2 Prepare the garnishes for the soup and serve them in small
bowls. Serve each helping of soup over half a cup of crushed ice
to keep it chilled or as here, straight from the fridge.

minestrone

THERE ARE MANY RECIPES FOR THIS CLASSIC DISH. THIS VERSION IS THICKENED WITH BOTH LENTILS AND SPAGHETTI AND MAKES A HEARTY APPETIZER. **SERVES 8**

1 large onion, finely chopped

1 large leek, trimmed and finely sliced

4 strips bacon, finely diced

2 Tbsp (25 mL) olive oil

1 cup (250 mL) finely diced carrot

⅓ cup (90 mL) red lentils

Two 14-fl oz (398-mL) cans chopped tomatoes

4 cups (1 L) rich vegetable or chicken stock

2 Tbsp (25 mL) freshly chopped herbs

Salt and freshly ground black pepper

¾ cup (175 mL) shredded cabbage

½ cup (125 mL) broken whole-wheat spaghetti

2 to 3 Tbsp (25 to 45 mL) pesto

1 Cook the onion, leek, and bacon in the oil until softened but not browned, then stir in the carrot and cook for a further 1 to 2 minutes. Add the lentils, tomatoes, stock, herbs, and seasonings and bring to a boil; cover the pan and simmer for 20 minutes.

2 Add the cabbage and spaghetti, return the soup to a boil, then simmer for a further 10 minutes. Season to taste, stir in the pesto, and serve immediately.

mulligatawny soup

MULLIGATAWNY COMES FROM THE TAMIL WORD "PEPPER WATER"; BEFORE CHILES WERE WIDELY AVAILABLE IN ASIA ALL THE HEAT IN CURRIES CAME FROM PEPPERCORNS. **SERVES 4 TO 6**

2 medium onions, finely sliced

3 Tbsp (45 mL) vegetable oil

1 chicken (about 3 lb/1.4 kg) jointed and skinned

1 to 2 Tbsp (15 to 25 mL) mild curry powder, according to taste

½ tsp (2 mL) ground cloves

⅔ cup (150 mL) plain yogurt

6 cups (1.5 L) water

1 tsp (5 mL) salt

Freshly ground black pepper

1 cup (250 mL) cooked rice

1 small tart red apple, cored and diced

Juice of ½ lemon

1 Cook the onion in the oil until soft then add the chicken pieces. Continue to cook over moderate heat until browned all over. Add the curry powder and ground cloves and cook for a further 1 minute, stir in the yogurt, and heat until the yogurt has loosened any scrapings from the bottom of the pot. Add the water to the pot with the salt and pepper, bring to a boil and simmer, covered, for 1 hour, or until the chicken begins to fall off the bone.

2 Remove the chicken, cut off the meat from the bone and return it to the pot with the cooked rice. Toss the apple in the lemon juice, add that to the pot, and return the soup to a boil. Simmer for 2 to 3 minutes, season to taste, and serve.

ABOVE THAI-SPICED CHICKEN CHOWDER

lebanese couscous soup

IN THIS RECIPE, COUSCOUS – TINY GRAINS MADE FROM SEMOLINA – IS USED TO THICKEN THE RICHLY SPICED ONION SOUP. **SERVES 6**

4 large onions, finely sliced

3 medium cloves garlic, finely sliced

2 Tbsp (25 mL) vegetable oil

1 Tbsp (15 mL) butter

1 small red chile, seeded and
    finely chopped

1 tsp (15 mL) mild chile powder

½ tsp (2 mL) ground turmeric

1 tsp (5 mL) ground coriander

8 cups (2 L) rich vegetable or
    chicken stock

Salt and freshly ground black pepper

⅓ cup (90 mL) couscous

Chopped fresh cilantro to garnish

1 Cook the onions and garlic in the oil and butter until well browned. This will take about 15 minutes over medium high heat. You must let the onions brown to achieve a rich color for the finished soup.

2 Stir in the chopped chile and the spices and cook over low heat for a further 1 to 2 minutes before adding the stock. Season lightly then bring to a boil. Cover and simmer for 30 minutes.

3 Stir the couscous into the soup, return to a boil, and simmer for a further 10 minutes. Season to taste then garnish with cilantro and serve immediately.

thai-spiced chicken chowder

PEEL THE LEMONGRASS AND BRUISE SLIGHTLY BEFORE FINELY CHOPPING. **SERVES 4**

1 to 2 Tbsp (15 to 25 mL) peanut or
    sunflower oil

2 small, boneless chicken breasts,
    skinned and shredded

2 tsp (10 mL) Thai 7-Spice seasoning

1 stick lemongrass, finely chopped

2 medium potatoes, diced

3 cups (750 mL) chicken or
    vegetable stock

2 cups (500 mL) milk

3 to 4 scallions, trimmed and
    finely sliced

1 cup (250 mL) frozen or fresh peas

1 to 2 Tbsp (15 to 25 mL) peanut
    sauce or peanut butter

Salt and freshly ground black pepper

Heavy cream to garnish (optional)

1 Heat the oil in a large pot; add the chicken and 7-Spice seasoning and cook quickly until the chicken begins to brown. Stir in the lemongrass and potato, then add the liquids. Bring the chowder slowly to a boil, cover, and simmer for 20 minutes.

2 Stir the scallions into the chowder with the peas; return to a boil and continue cooking for a further 5 minutes.

3 Add the peanut sauce to the chowder just before serving. Remove from heat and stir until melted. Season to taste and serve, garnished with a spoonful of cream if desired.

chicken and bean chowder

THIS MAKES FOR A MEAL IN ITSELF WHEN SERVED WITH CRUSTY BREAD AND A FRESH
GREEN SALAD. **SERVES 6**

2 Tbsp (25 mL) olive oil

2 medium chicken thighs

1 large onion, finely chopped

**1 medium green bell pepper, seeded
and cut into strips**

**1 small red chile, seeded and finely
chopped**

2 small cloves garlic, crushed

**1 Tbsp (15 mL) chopped fresh
oregano**

**1 Tbsp (15 mL) chopped fresh
flat-leafed parsley**

**14-fl oz (398-mL) can chopped
tomatoes**

2 Tbsp (25 mL) tomato paste

**5 cups (1.25 L) rich chicken or
vegetable stock**

Salt and freshly ground black pepper

**15-oz (425-g) can borlotti beans or
mixed legumes, drained and rinsed**

**Chopped fresh parsley and Parmesan
cheese to garnish**

1 Heat the oil in a large pot; add the chicken and brown all over. Remove the chicken from the pot with a slotted spoon and set aside. Stir the onion into the pot juices and cook until softened but not browned. Add the pepper, chile, garlic, and herbs and stir well. Add the tomatoes, tomato paste, and stock. Return the chicken to the pot, season lightly, and bring the soup to a boil. Cover and simmer for 40 to 50 minutes, until the chicken is cooked.

2 Remove the chicken from the pot and cut off the meat from the bones. Shred the chicken and return it to the pot with the beans. Return the soup to a boil and simmer for 3 to 4 minutes to heat the beans thoroughly.

3 Season the soup to taste and garnish with extra parsley. Slivers of Parmesan cheese may be sprinkled into the soup before serving.

squash chowder

USE ANY HARD-SKINNED SQUASH FOR THIS CHOWDER. JUST REMEMBER: THE SMOOTHER SKINNED THE SQUASH, THE EASIER IT IS TO PEEL! **SERVES 6**

3 cups (750 mL) squash, diced finely

2 strips bacon, finely chopped

2 Tbsp (25 mL) fruity olive oil

4 to 5 sprigs fresh thyme

2 bay leaves

4 cups (1 L) rich vegetable stock

Salt and freshly ground black pepper

1 cup (250 mL) cabbage, finely shredded

2 oz (60 g) cream of coconut

1 cup (250 mL) milk

1 large tomato, finely diced

1 cup (250 mL) frozen or fresh shrimp (optional)

1 Tbsp (15 mL) white wine vinegar

Chopped fresh parsley to garnish

1 Cook the squash and the bacon in the oil in a heavy pan for 6 to 8 minutes, stirring frequently, until the squash is beginning to soften. Add the herbs and stock, season lightly, and bring to a boil. Reduce the heat and simmer for 10 minutes, then add the cabbage and cream of coconut and continue cooking for a further 10 to 15 minutes.

2 Remove the thyme and bay leaves, then add the milk and the chopped tomato with the shrimp, if desired. Return the chowder to a boil and cook for a further 5 minutes. Season to taste, then add the vinegar and parsley just before serving.

smoked fish chowder

FIRM-FLESHED SMOKED FISH MAKES AN EXCELLENT CHOWDER.

SERVES 6

2 cups (500 mL) milk

8 oz (250 g) smoked haddock or other white fish fillet, skinned

1 Tbsp (15 mL) butter

1 small onion, finely chopped

2 sticks celery, finely chopped

2 medium potatoes, diced

2 cups (500 mL) fish stock or water

1 cup (250 mL) frozen or fresh peas

1 cup (250 mL) frozen corn

Salt and freshly ground black pepper

2 Tbsp (25 mL) chopped fresh parsley

1 Heat the milk in a skillet until almost boiling, then add the haddock and poach for 4 to 5 minutes. Remove the haddock with a slotted spoon and reserve the milk.

2 Melt the butter in a separate pan, add the onion and celery and cook slowly until soft. Stir in the diced potato, stock, and the reserved milk and bring to a boil. Reduce the heat and simmer the soup for 15 minutes, until the potato is tender.

3 Add the peas and corn and return the soup to a boil. Flake the haddock and add it to the chowder, then continue to cook for a further 2 to 3 minutes, until the peas and corn are tender and the fish is hot.

4 Season the chowder to taste and stir in half the parsley. Garnish with the remaining parsley and serve.

51

buckwheat and mushroom soup

BUCKWHEAT HAS A STRONG, SLIGHTLY SWEET AND FRAGRANTLY NUTTY FLAVOR. ONLY A LITTLE IS REQUIRED SO AS NOT TO OVERPOWER THE MUSHROOMS. **SERVES 6**

½ cup (125 mL) dried porcini
  mushrooms

½ cup (125 mL) sherry

1 Tbsp (15 mL) butter

1 Tbsp (15 mL) olive oil

1 large onion, finely chopped

2 sticks celery, finely chopped

2 strips bacon, finely chopped

3 cups (750 mL) roughly chopped
  mushrooms

2 plump cloves garlic, finely sliced

¼ cup (60 mL) raw buckwheat groats

5 cups (1.25 L) rich vegetable stock

Salt and freshly ground black pepper

Nutmeg

1 cup (250 mL) milk

Cream and paprika to garnish

1 Soak the porcinis in the sherry for at least 30 minutes before starting the soup. Heat the butter and the oil together then add the onion, celery, and bacon and cook slowly for about 5 minutes, until the vegetables have softened but not browned. Add the chopped mushrooms and garlic and cook slowly for a further 2 to 3 minutes, until the juices start to run from the mushrooms. Add the porcinis and the sherry, then stir in the buckwheat and pour in the stock.

2 Bring the soup slowly to a boil, stirring up any scrapings from the bottom of the pot. Season lightly with salt, pepper, and nutmeg, then cover the pot and simmer the soup for 40 minutes.

3 Allow the soup to cool slightly then purée until smooth in a blender or food processor. Rinse the pot and return the soup to it with the milk. Reheat gently, then season to taste. Garnish with a swirl of cream and a little paprika.

crab and sweet corn soup

THIS IS A CLASSIC CHINESE SOUP WITH A CREAMY, FRAGRANT COMBINATION OF FLAVORS. **SERVES 6**

15-oz (425-g) can creamed corn

8-oz (250-g) can or fresh crab meat

5 cups (1.25 L) rich fish, chicken, or
  vegetable stock

Salt and freshly ground black pepper

1 Tbsp (15 mL) soy sauce

2 egg whites

4 to 6 scallions, shredded

1 Bring the corn, crab meat, stock, seasoning, and soy sauce to a boil in a large pot, stirring to mix the corn and the crab evenly throughout the soup. Simmer for 10 minutes.

2 Whisk the egg whites into soft peaks, then stir carefully into the soup just before serving. Garnish with scallions.

chickpea soup with red pepper salsa

DON'T BE PUT OFF BY THE NUMBER OF INGREDIENTS – THIS IS A LIGHTLY SPICED, CREAMY SOUP WITH A ZINGY
SALSA GARNISH – DELICIOUS! **SERVES 6**

¾ **cup (175 mL) chickpeas, soaked
overnight or canned**

1 tsp (5 mL) cumin seeds

½ **tsp (2 mL) mustard seeds,
preferably white**

1 Tbsp (15 mL) sesame seeds

1 large onion, finely sliced

1 Tbsp (15 mL) olive oil

2 large cloves garlic, finely sliced

½ **tsp (2 mL) dry ground ginger**

4 cups (1 L) rich stock

Salt and freshly ground black pepper

1 cup (250 mL) milk

SALSA

½ **small red bell pepper, chopped**

¼ **cucumber, chopped**

½ **small red onion, finely chopped**

1 medium clove garlic, finely chopped

1 small tomato, chopped

**1 small red chile, seeded and
finely chopped**

1 to 2 Tbsp cilantro leaves, finely torn

Grated rind and juice of 1 lemon

**1 to 2 Tbsp (15 to 25 mL) sour cream
(optional)**

1 Drain the chickpeas and rinse them thoroughly under cold running water; set aside. Heat a non-stick skillet until evenly hot, add the cumin, mustard, and sesame seeds and roast for 2 to 3 minutes, until they start to pop. Transfer the spices to a mortar or a spice mill and grind until smooth. You may also use the end of a rolling pin to grind them.

2 Cook the onion in the oil in a large pot until well browned, then add the garlic, ginger, and freshly ground spices and cook slowly for another minute. Stir in the chickpeas, and the stock and bring the soup to a boil; season lightly. Simmer for 45 to 60 minutes, until the chickpeas are soft.

3 Prepare the salsa while the soup is cooking. Mix together all the prepared vegetables, season lightly and add the cilantro, lemon rind, and lemon juice. Allow the salsa to stand for at least 30 minutes for the flavors to blend together.

4 Allow the soup to cool slightly, then purée in a blender or food processor until smooth. Rinse the pot and return the soup to it, reheat gently with the milk, seasoning with salt and pepper to taste. Blend the salsa with 1 to 2 Tbsp (15 to 25 mL) of sour cream, if wished, and serve the soup with a generous spoonful of salsa over each portion.

roasted pumpkin and smoked mussel soup

IF YOU CANNOT FIND SMOKED MUSSELS, WARMED SMOKED MACKEREL WILL MAKE A
DELICIOUS SUBSTITUTE. **SERVES 6**

½ small pumpkin or 1 medium firm-
   fleshed squash

Freshly ground black pepper

3 Tbsp (45 mL) olive oil

1 medium leek, finely sliced

2 sticks celery, trimmed and sliced

1 small carrot, sliced

2 tsp (10 mL) ground coriander

3 to 4 sprigs fresh thyme

1 bay leaf

4 cups (1 L) rich vegetable stock

2 cups (500 mL) milk

Salt

1 cup (500 mL) smoked mussels

Chopped fresh parsley

1 Preheat oven to 425°F (220°C). Cut the pumpkin into slices about 1½ to 2 in (4 to 5 cm) wide and place them in a roasting pan. You will need 6 slices. Season lightly with pepper then brush the flesh with olive oil. Bake in the preheated oven for about 30 minutes, until the pumpkin is tender. Scoop the flesh from the skin and place to one side.

2 Heat 2 Tbsp (25 mL) of olive oil in a large pot; add the leek, celery, and carrot and cook slowly until soft. Stir in the ground coriander and cook slowly for a further minute. Add the pumpkin flesh to the pot with the thyme and bay leaf, then pour in the stock. Bring the soup to a boil, cover and simmer slowly for 35 to 40 minutes.

3 Allow the soup to cool slightly then purée until smooth in a blender or food processor. Rinse the pot, then return the soup to it with the milk and bring slowly to simmering point. Season well with salt and pepper, add the smoked mussels, and heat for another minute or two. Serve garnished with parsley.

leek and spinach barley soup

LEEKS GREW WILD IN IRELAND FOR MANY CENTURIES. HERE THEY ADD
TO THE TRADITIONAL FLAVOR OF THIS WARMING SOUP. **SERVES 6**

3 cups (750 mL) finely sliced leeks

2 Tbsp (25 mL) olive oil

¾ cup (175 mL) shredded spinach

⅓ cup (90 mL) pearl barley

6 cups (1.5 L) rich chicken or vegetable stock

1 bouquet garni

Salt and freshly ground black pepper

2 bay leaves

¼ cup (60 mL) heavy cream (optional)

1 Cook the leeks in the oil until softened but not browned, then
add the spinach and cook briefly until wilted. Add the barley,
stock, and bouquet garni, and bring to a boil. Season lightly, add
the bay leaves, then cover the pot and simmer for about 1½ hours,
until the barley is tender.

2 Remove the bouquet garni and bay leaves. Season to taste,
then stir in the cream, if used, and serve immediately with
fresh crusty bread.

2 Salads and appetizers

Many of the salads included in this section are suitable as a side dish or as a main course with hot potatoes or crusty bread. If you are planning to serve a salad as a main course you will usually need to double the quantities.

Salads have come a long way in the last few years, and designer lettuces and other unusual greens offer all sorts of presentation opportunities for the home cook. While the appearance of a salad is very important, the selection of the ingredients, which should all be at the very peak of their ripeness, is paramount. It is impossible to make a good salad from limp lettuce, underripe tomatoes, and a hard, tasteless strawberry added for a touch of sophistication. Some of the best salads are made from the simplest of ingredients, all packed with flavor. The Spinach Salad included here is an excellent example of a very simple dish based on fresh and flavorful ingredients: young spinach and sun-ripened tomatoes.

I always like to use a full-flavored homemade dressing for my salads, usually made with a fruity extra-virgin olive oil. I use sherry vinegar and a generous amount of mustard, balanced with sugar, salt, and pepper. Taste the dressing, then keep adding seasonings until it is right.

Appetizers should always be small and fairly light. They should stimulate the appetite for what is to follow and never be too filling or too heavy. Do not serve a very heavily seasoned dish before a delicate main course, which may seem bland in comparison, but try to pick dishes that complement each other.

LEFT CRUNCHY CORN SALAD (SEE PAGE 64)

pasta salad

USE WHITE PASTA IF YOU PREFER, THERE IS PLENTY OF FIBER IN THE VEGETABLES AND BEANS. **SERVES 12 AS AN APPETIZER, 6 TO 8 AS A MAIN COURSE**

8 oz (250 g) whole-wheat pasta of your choice

1 medium red bell pepper, seeded and diced

1½ cups (375 mL) button mushrooms, halved

1 cup (250 mL) diced cucumber

1½ cups (375 mL) corn

6 scallions, finely sliced

15-oz (425-g) can red kidney beans, drained and rinsed

1 cup (250 mL) diced Swiss cheese

Salt and freshly ground black pepper

DRESSING

1½ cups (375 mL) strained cottage cheese or plain yogurt

1 cup (250 mL) mayonnaise

Salt and freshly ground black pepper

2 to 3 cloves garlic, crushed

⅓ cup (90 mL) chopped fresh chives

Salad greens to serve

1 Bring a large pot of salted water to a boil and add the pasta. Return to a boil, then simmer as directed until just tender. Drain the pasta and rinse it in cold water, then let cool completely.

2 Mix all the prepared vegetables together and season lightly with salt and pepper. Blend all the ingredients for the dressing and season to taste.

3 Place the pasta in a large bowl, then top with the vegetables. Spoon on the dressing. If the salad is prepared in advance, I suggest leaving it in layers and tossing at the last minute. If it is to be served immediately, however, toss all the ingredients together then transfer the salad to a large platter, lined with salad greens.

roasted endive and pink grapefruit salad

I LOVE ENDIVE, BUT I PREFER IT COOKED TO RAW. HERE IT IS SET OFF BY THE ZING OF THE GRAPEFRUIT. **SERVES 4**

2 heads endive, trimmed

1 Tbsp (15 mL) finely chopped onion

Salt and freshly ground black pepper

1 Tbsp (15 mL) olive oil

⅓ cup (90 mL) pine nuts

2 medium tomatoes, halved and sliced

1 small ruby red grapefruit, peeled and cut into segments

1 to 2 Tbsp (15 to 25 mL) chopped fresh chives

Salt and freshly ground black pepper

1 to 2 Tbsp (15 to 25 mL) fruity olive oil

1 Preheat the oven to 425°F (220°C). Cut the endive in half lengthways and place in a roasting tin. Scatter the onion over top, season well and drizzle with the oil. Roast in the preheated oven for 15 minutes, then allow to cool.

2 Toast the pine nuts in a hot dry skillet for 3 to 4 minutes until browned, then allow to cool.

3 Slice the roasted endive and mix it with the pine nuts, tomatoes, grapefruit, and chives. Season well, spoon the olive oil over, then serve on a bed of lettuce or raw spinach.

classic waldorf salad

MIXING YOGURT WITH MAYONNAISE MAKES A MUCH MILDER DRESSING FOR THE SALAD. **SERVES 6 TO 8**

2 small Red Delicious apples, cored and diced

2 small Granny Smith apples, cored and diced

Juice of 1 lemon

1 head celery, trimmed and sliced

2 cups (500 mL) chopped walnuts

Salt and freshly ground black pepper

1 cup (250 mL) plain yogurt

½ cup (125 mL) mayonnaise

Lettuce leaves

Paprika

1 Toss the diced apples in the lemon juice to prevent them from browning. Mix the apples with the celery and walnuts and season well.

2 Blend the yogurt and mayonnaise together, then spoon over the salad. Toss until all the ingredients are evenly coated; add extra mayonnaise if necessary.

3 Line a bowl with lettuce leaves, then arrange the salad in the bowl. Sprinkle a little paprika over the salad just before serving.

pear and grape salad

THIS SALAD OFFERS A DELICIOUS COMBINATION OF TASTES AND TEXTURES. **SERVES 4**

2 heads Boston lettuce, torn into bite-sized pieces

1 head endive, trimmed and sliced

2 large ripe dessert pears, sliced

Juice of ½ lemon

2 cups (500 mL) grapes, preferably black, halved and seeded

½ cup (125 mL) sour cream

⅓ cup (90 mL) low-fat cream cheese

1 to 2 cloves garlic, crushed

Salt and freshly ground black pepper

Paprika

1 Mix together the lettuce and endive and arrange in a salad bowl or on individual plates. Toss the pears in the lemon juice, arrange the pieces over the lettuce, and add the grapes.

2 Blend together the sour cream and cream cheese, add the garlic, and season well with salt and pepper. Spoon the dressing into the center of the salad, garnish with paprika, then serve with fresh, crusty whole-wheat bread.

crunchy corn salad

IF YOU PREFER, BLANCH THE BEAN SPROUTS BEFORE ADDING THEM
TO THE SALAD. **SERVES 4**

4 oz (125 g) fresh corn, cut from the cob

4 oz (125 g) snow peas, trimmed and julienned

1 medium zucchini, julienned

1 large carrot, julienned

2 pieces preserved stem ginger, chopped

1 cup (250 mL) bean sprouts

2 Tbsp (25 mL) sesame seeds, toasted

DRESSING

2 Tbsp (25 mL) liquid honey

1 Tbsp (15 mL) sesame oil

Grated rind and juice of 1 lime

2 Tbsp (25 mL) ginger syrup (from the bottle of preserved ginger)

2 Tbsp (25 mL) light soy sauce

Salt and freshly ground black pepper

1 Blanch the corn in a large pan of water for just 2 minutes, then add the snow peas and cook for 1 minute. Drain the vegetables, then plunge immediately into cold water. Drain again when cold.

2 Combine the blanched vegetables with the zucchini and carrot, ginger, and bean sprouts, then add the sesame seeds.

3 Whisk together all the ingredients for the dressing and season to taste with salt and pepper. Pour the dressing over the salad vegetables and toss thoroughly before serving.

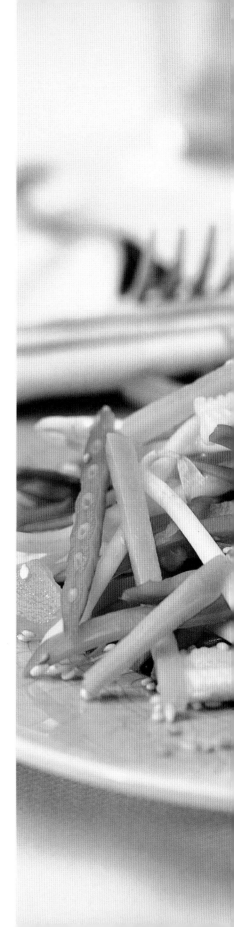

buckwheat salad

BUCKWHEAT IS USED EXTENSIVELY IN EASTERN EUROPEAN COOKERY. ROASTING THE GROATS BRINGS OUT THE NUTTY FLAVOR. **SERVES 6 TO 8**

1 cup (250 mL) buckwheat groats, roasted or raw

3 cups (650 mL) rich vegetable stock

3 Tbsp (45 mL) vinaigrette

1 cup (250 mL) diced carrot

½ cup (125 mL) diced cucumber

⅓ cup (90 mL) diced pickles

⅓ cup (90 mL) poppy seeds

⅓ cup (90 mL) chopped fresh parsley (optional)

Salt and freshly ground black pepper

1 Bring the buckwheat and stock to a boil, cover the pot and simmer for 30 to 35 minutes until the stock has been absorbed and the groats are tender. Drain any excess liqiud. Stir in the vinaigrette, then leave to cool completely.

2 Add all the remaining ingredients to the buckwheat and mix well, seasoning to taste. Serve at room temperature.

brown rice salad with fruit and seeds

TRY ADDING STRAWBERRIES WHEN THEY ARE IN SEASON. **SERVES 6**

1½ cups (625 mL) brown rice

⅓ cup (90 mL) sunflower seeds

¼ cup (60 mL) sesame seeds

⅓ cup (90 mL) pumpkin seeds

6 scallions, trimmed and sliced

1 large mango, peeled and diced

⅓ cup (90 mL) dried cranberries

DRESSING

Grated rind and juice of 1 lemon

2 Tbsp (25 mL) liquid honey

4 Tbsp (50 mL) sunflower or peanut oil

1 Tbsp (15 mL) dill weed, chopped

Salt and freshly ground black pepper

1 Bring the rice to a boil in a large pot of cold water and simmer for 20 to 25 minutes until the rice is just tender but not soggy.

2 Prepare the dressing while the rice is cooking. Whisk together all the ingredients, seasoning to taste with salt and pepper. Drain the rice well, shake gently, then transfer it to a large bowl and add the dressing. Toss well and leave until the rice has cooled, tossing from time to time.

3 Toast the sunflower seeds in a dry skillet for 2 to 3 minutes until they begin to brown, then add the sesame seeds and cook for a further 1 to 2 minutes. Allow to cool, then add the pumpkin seeds.

4 Toss the cooled rice with the seeds, scallions, and fruit. Add a little extra seasoning if necessary and garnish with more dill just before serving.

cucumber tabbouleh

IT IS IMPORTANT TO DRY THE BULGUR THOROUGHLY OR THE FINISHED SALAD WILL BE SOGGY. **SERVES 6**

1 cup (250 mL) bulgur

2 cups (500 mL) boiling water

⅓ cup (90 mL) chopped fresh parsley

⅓ cup (90 mL) chopped fresh mint

2 medium tomatoes, seeded and chopped

2 scallions, trimmed and finely chopped

1⅓ cups (340 mL) diced cucumber

Juice of 1 lime

Salt and freshly ground black pepper

¼ cup (60 mL) fruity olive oil

1 Allow the bulgur to soak in boiling water for 30 minutes, then drain, and squeeze dry in a clean dish towel.

2 Place the bulgur in a large bowl and add all the remaining ingredients, including seasonings to taste. Toss the salad well and serve at room temperature.

cracked wheat salad

SLICE THE VEGETABLES QUITE FINELY SO THAT THEY DO NOT
CONTRAST TOO WILDLY WITH THE WHEAT. **SERVES 6 TO 8**

1 cup (250 mL) cracked wheat or kamut

2 cups (500 mL) boiling water

⅓ cup (90 mL) pumpkin seeds

1 small green bell pepper, seeded and finely chopped

2 sticks celery, finely sliced

1 small leek, trimmed and finely sliced

½ small cucumber, finely diced

1 cup (250 mL) chopped fresh parsley

⅓ cup (90 mL) chopped fresh mixed herbs

DRESSING

Grated rind and juice of 1 lime

¼ cup (60 mL) fruity extra-virgin olive oil

Salt and freshly ground black pepper

1 Place the cracked wheat in a bowl, pour the boiling water over, and leave for at least 30 minutes. Drain in a sieve, then wring excess water out in a clean dish towel.

2 Place the cracked wheat in a bowl with the seeds and prepared vegetables. Season lightly.

3 Whisk the dressing ingredients until blended, then pour it over the salad. Top with a layer of the freshly chopped herbs, all mixed together. Toss all the ingredients just before serving.

date and pear cottage cheese salad

THE ADVANTAGE OF COTTAGE CHEESE OVER OTHER CHEESES IS THAT IT IS LOW IN FAT. **SERVES 4**

1 cup (250 mL) cottage cheese

½ cup (125 mL) pitted dates,
    chopped

2 medium firm dessert pears

Juice of 1 lemon

2 small oranges

2 heads endive, trimmed and sliced

Salt and freshly ground black pepper

Watercress or arugula leaves

1 Place the cottage cheese in a bowl and add the dates. Core and dice the pears and toss with the lemon juice. Peel the oranges and cut the rind into thin strips for garnish. Remove any seeds, then roughly chop the oranges. Add the pears to the cottage cheese with the oranges, and endive. Season to taste with salt and pepper.

2 Line a suitable bowl or platter with watercress or arugula leaves, then arrange the salad in the middle. Garnish with the reserved orange rind before serving.

beet and sorrel salad

ADD THE BEETS JUST BEFORE SERVING TO PREVENT THEIR COLOR FROM BLEEDING INTO THE OTHER INGREDIENTS. **SERVES 4**

Salad greens

1 small bunch watercress, trimmed,
    washed, and shaken dry

1 cup (250 mL) shredded young
    sorrel or spinach leaves

1 cup (250 mL) shredded celeriac
    (celery root) or thinly sliced celery

Grated rind and juice of 1 lemon

4 small beets, cooked and diced

DRESSING

4 Tbsp (50 mL) fruity olive oil

1 Tbsp (15 mL) sherry vinegar

½ tsp (2 mL) sugar

1 Tbsp (15 mL) Dijon mustard

Salt and freshly ground black pepper

1 Arrange the salad leaves in a bowl or on a platter, then add the watercress and sorrel and mix well. Toss the celeriac with the lemon rind and juice (to prevent discoloration) and add to the salad with the diced beets.

2 Whisk all the ingredients for the dressing together; the mustard will make the dressing quite thick. Pour over the salad, toss and serve immediately.

new potatoes niçoise

A SALAD NIÇOISE USUALLY FEATURES TUNA, BUT I HAVE USED ANCHOVIES AND NEW POTATOES, FRESHLY COOKED AND STILL WARM IN THEIR SKINS. **SERVES 6 TO 8**

1 lb (450 g) small new potatoes, scrubbed

Salad greens

4 medium tomatoes, cut into wedges

¾ cup (175 mL) cold cooked fava beans

4 hard-boiled eggs, quartered

2 Tbsp (25 mL) chopped fresh mixed herbs

½ cup (125 mL) small black olives

Salt and freshly ground black pepper

2-oz (60-g) can anchovy fillets

2 Tbsp (25 mL) butter

1 Bring the potatoes to a boil in a pot of water, then simmer for 10 to 12 minutes, or until just cooked.

2 Prepare the salad while the potatoes are cooking. Cover the bottom of a large bowl or platter with the salad greens, then arrange the tomatoes, fava beans, and hard-boiled eggs around the edge. Sprinkle the salad with the herbs and olives, then season lightly with salt and pepper. Cut the anchovy fillets in half lengthwise and arrange the pieces over the salad, reserving the oil.

3 Drain the potatoes and return them to the pot. Add the butter, tossing the potatoes until it has melted, then arrange the potatoes in the center of the salad. Add the oil from the anchovies to the butter left in the pan, stir in a few grinds of pepper, then pour the mixture over the salad and serve immediately.

spinach salad

⅓ cup (90 mL) pine nuts

4 handfuls young spinach leaves,
washed and dried

2 handfuls arugula

1 cup (250 mL) cherry tomatoes,
halved

Shavings of fresh Parmesan cheese

Salt and freshly ground black pepper

4 to 5 Tbsp (45 to 65 mL) garlic
vinaigrette

1 Heat a nonstick skillet until evenly hot; add the pine nuts and cook until golden brown on both sides, shaking the pan almost continuously to stop the nuts from burning. Allow the nuts to cool on paper towels.

2 Mix the spinach and arugula together in a large, flat dish, tearing the arugula into bite-sized pieces. Add the tomatoes and pine nuts, then add Parmesan cheese to taste; an easy way to cut the shavings is with a potato peeler.

3 Season the salad lightly with salt and pepper, then add the vinaigrette and toss before serving.

summer couscous salad

REMOVE THE PEPPER SKINS AFTER ROASTING BY PEELING FROM THE FLOWER END. **SERVES 6**

2 medium red bell peppers

3 to 4 small chiles

2 cups (500 mL) couscous

⅔ cup (150 mL) pine nuts, toasted

1 cup (250 mL) finely sliced button
  mushrooms

1 small zucchini, finely chopped

3 Tbsp (45 mL) vinaigrette or extra-
  virgin olive oil

Salt and freshly ground black pepper

1 Tbsp (15 mL) chopped fresh parsley

1 small avocado, sliced and tossed in
  lemon juice

1 Preheat the oven to 400°F (200°C). Place the bell peppers and the chiles on a baking sheet and roast in the oven for 20 to 40 minutes, turning once during cooking. The chiles may only take 20 minutes to blacken and should be removed as soon as they are ready. Cover the hot peppers with a damp dish towel and leave until cool. Peel, discard the core and seeds, and chop the flesh.

2 Cover the couscous with boiling water and allow it to stand for at least 20 minutes; add a little more water if it seems dry, but do not drown the grains. Drain well. Add the roasted peppers and all the remaining ingredients, except the avocado, and toss thoroughly. Transfer to a bowl or platter and garnish with the avocado just before serving.

lentil salad

LENTILS AND CURRY ARE ALWAYS A NATURALLY DELICIOUS COMBINATION. **SERVES 4 TO 6**

15-oz (425-g) can green lentils,
  drained and rinsed, or ¾ cup
  (175 mL) freshly cooked lentils

1 cup (250 mL) grated carrot

2 sticks celery, finely chopped

⅓ cup (90 mL) golden raisins

1 Tbsp (15 mL) chopped cilantro

DRESSING

3 Tbsp (45 mL) sunflower oil

1 Tbsp (15 mL) white wine vinegar

½ tsp (2 mL) curry powder

Salt and freshly ground black pepper

1 Combine all the salad ingredients in a bowl. Whisk together the oil and vinegar for the dressing, add the curry powder, then season to taste.

2 Pour the dressing into the bowl, toss the salad well, then chill lightly for about 30 minutes before serving.

rice and pistachio salad

THIS SALAD IS THICKENED WITH A HONEY DRESSING. **SERVES 4 TO 6**

1½ cups (375 mL) wild and white rice mix

½ cup (125 mL) raisins

½ cup (125 mL) pistachios, shelled and unsalted

4 scallions, trimmed and sliced

4 medium tomatoes, chopped

DRESSING

¼ cup (60 mL) liquid honey

1 Tbsp (15 mL) cider vinegar

Grated rind and juice of 1 lemon

2 Tbsp (25 mL) olive oil

Salt and freshly ground black pepper

1 Tbsp (15 mL) chopped fresh chives

1 Bring both types of rice to a boil in plenty of water, then cover and simmer for 20 minutes. While the rice is cooking, whisk all the ingredients for the dressing together and season to taste. Drain the rice thoroughly, then add the dressing and toss it with the grains. Transfer the rice to a bowl and allow it to cool completely.

2 Add the remaining ingredients to the salad and stir them carefully into the rice. Season to taste with extra salt and pepper before serving.

baby lima bean and tuna salad

THIS RECIPE IS BASED ON ITALIAN ANTIPASTO. **SERVES 3 TO 4**

15-oz (425-g) can baby lima beans, drained and rinsed

3½-oz (100-g) can tuna, drained

1 small red onion, finely sliced

1 to 2 small cloves garlic, finely sliced

2 ripe medium tomatoes, seeded and chopped

1 Tbsp (15 mL) capers

Salt and freshly ground black pepper

3 Tbsp (45 mL) olive oil

1 Tbsp (15 mL) chopped parsley

Lemon wedge, to serve

Small romaine lettuce leaves, optional

3 hard-boiled eggs, optional

1 Place the beans in a bowl. Flake the tuna and add it to the beans with the onion, garlic, tomatoes, and capers. Stir in seasoning to taste, then moisten the salad with olive oil.

2 Sprinkle with chopped parsley and serve with a lemon wedge. You can also serve with romaine lettuce leaves and wedges of hard-boiled egg if desired.

mushroom and hazelnut pâté

A FLAVORFUL VEGETARIAN PÂTÉ – SERVE WITH SALAD GREENS. **SERVES 6 TO 8**

1½ cups (375 mL) hazelnuts, toasted and chopped

1½ cups (375 mL) fresh whole-wheat bread crumbs, tightly packed

1 medium onion

2 plump cloves garlic

1 lb (450 g) mushrooms, trimmed

4 Tbsp (50 mL) butter

Salt and freshly ground black pepper

2 Tbsp (25 mL) soy sauce

1 large egg, beaten

2 thin strips bacon (optional)

1 Preheat the oven to 350°F (175°C). Combine the hazelnuts with the bread crumbs in a bowl. Finely chop the onion, garlic, and mushrooms – this is best done in a food processor.

2 Melt the butter in a large skillet, add the mushroom mixture, and cook slowly for about 5 minutes, until the juices run from the mushrooms. Allow to cool slightly, then add to the hazelnut mixture with plenty of salt, pepper, and the soy sauce. Blend together with the beaten egg.

3 Lightly grease a small loaf pan. Stretch the bacon with the back of a knife, then arrange it in the base of the pan. Spoon the hazelnut mixture into the pan and smooth the top. Cover with greased foil and place in a shallow roasting pan. Half-fill the roasting pan with hot water.

4 Bake in the preheated oven for 1 hour, then remove the pâté from the roasting pan and allow to cool. Chill the pâté overnight in the refrigerator, then loosen it with a knife and turn out onto a serving plate. Serve with salad greens.

wild rice-stuffed mushrooms

ONE MUSHROOM PER PERSON MAKES AN AMPLE APPETIZER. **SERVES 4**

⅓ cup wild rice

1 cup finely chopped watercress

⅔ cup low-fat cottage cheese

4 scallions, trimmed and chopped

Salt and freshly ground black pepper

4 large field mushrooms, peeled

Olive oil

Paprika

4 slices freshly cooked whole-wheat toast

1 Bring the rice to a boil in a pan of water, then simmer for 30 to 40 minutes until tender. Drain thoroughly and allow to cool slightly.

2 Mix the rice with the chopped watercress, cottage cheese, and scallions; season to taste. Preheat broiler. Remove the stems from the mushrooms and brush the shells lightly with oil. Heat for 3 to 4 minutes under the hot broiler until almost cooked. Arrange the filling in the mushroom shells, and cook for a further 3 to 4 minutes, until the filling is set and hot. Sprinkle a little paprika over the mushrooms and serve immediately on hot, lightly buttered whole-wheat toast.

tortilla wheels with pineapple salsa

THESE MINI TORTILLAS ARE GREAT APPETIZERS. **SERVES 6 TO 8**

FILLING

¾ cup (175 mL) cream cheese

1 medium green chile, seeded and finely chopped

2 Tbsp (25 mL) chopped fresh cilantro

4 medium tomatoes, seeded and finely chopped

4 scallions, finely chopped

1 medium bell pepper, red or yellow, seeded and finely chopped

1 cup (250 mL) grated Cheddar cheese

Salt and freshly ground black pepper

8 flour tortillas

SALSA

1 Tbsp (15 mL) black or brown mustard seeds

1 medium orange

4 thick slices pineapple, fresh or canned

1 small red onion, finely chopped

1 small green chile, seeded and finely chopped

2 small tomatoes, diced

1 Beat the cream cheese until smooth, then add all the other ingredients for the filling. Mix well and season to taste with salt and pepper. Divide the mixture between the tortillas, spreading evenly. Place each tortilla flat on top of another, making 4 stacks of 2, then roll them up tightly. Cover in plastic wrap and chill for at least 2 hours.

2 Prepare the salsa while the tortilla rolls are chilling. Heat a nonstick skillet until evenly hot, then add the mustard seeds and cook for 1 to 2 minutes, until the seeds begin to pop. Allow to cool. Grate the rind from the orange, set aside. Peel the orange and chop the flesh. Mix the orange and rind with the mustard seeds and all the other ingredients, seasoning to taste with salt and pepper. Let the salsa stand until required.

3 Preheat the oven to 400°F (200°C). Unwrap the tortillas and trim away the ends. Cut each roll into 8 slices. Place flat on baking sheets and bake in the hot oven for 15 to 20 minutes, until well-browned. Serve hot with the salsa.

apricot, almond and tomato salad

THIS SALAD PAIRS PERFECTLY WITH CURRIED VEGETABLE CASSEROLE
(SEE PAGE 118). **SERVES 4 TO 6**

¾ cup (175 mL) blanched almonds

Salt

Cayenne pepper

Salad greens

4 medium ripe tomatoes, cut into wedges

1 cup (250 mL) dried apricots, chopped

6 Tbsp (75 mL) mustard vinaigrette

Parsley

1 Heat a skillet, preferably nonstick, until evenly hot, then add
the almonds. Cook over moderate heat until evenly browned on
both sides (the almonds may be toasted if preferred). Dust some
paper towels with salt and cayenne pepper, then add the hot
almonds and toss until well-coated with the seasonings. Allow to
cool, tossing from time to time.

2 Line a platter or bowl with some of the salad greens. Mix
together the tomatoes, chopped apricots, and deviled almonds,
and the rest of the salad greens of your choice and arrange on the
platter. Spoon on the mustard vinaigrette and garnish with a
sprig of parsley.

ABOVE WARM JALAPEÑO BEAN DIP

brie quesadillas

THESE MEXICAN-STYLE SNACKS CAN BE EATEN AS EITHER AN APPETIZER OR A LIGHT MEAL. **SERVES 6 TO 8**

Flour tortillas

FOR EACH TORTILLA

2 to 3 Tbsp (15 to 25 mL) refried beans

1½ oz (40 g) ripe Brie, cut into slivers

Chopped avocado, pickled jalapeños, and tomato salsa

1 Spread half of each tortilla with the refried beans, then top with the brie. Preheat a nonstick skillet and add the tortilla. Shake over the heat until the cheese begins to melt.

2 Meanwhile, preheat the broiler. Finish heating the tortilla through under the broiler, until the cheese has melted and the beans are hot. If possible keep the uncovered tortilla away from the heat to prevent it from becoming crispy.

3 Top the cheese with avocado, jalapeño slices, and tomato salsa, then fold the quesadilla in half to serve.

warm jalapeño bean dip

REFRIED BEANS – MASHED PINTO BEANS – ARE A STAPLE OF THE MEXICAN DIET. THEY ARE SERVED HERE ENLIVENED BY THE TANG OF CHILE. **SERVES 8**

4 scallions, finely chopped

1 small jalapeño chile, seeded and finely chopped

1 medium clove garlic, crushed

1 Tbsp (15 mL) olive oil

1 lb (450 g) refried beans

1 Tbsp (15 mL) chopped cilantro

2 small tomatoes, finely chopped

⅔ cup (150 mL) sour cream

Salt

1 Cook the scallions, chile, and garlic in the oil until softened but not browned. Add the refried beans and heat gently for 2 or 3 minutes before adding the cilantro, tomatoes, and sour cream.

2 Mix carefully and continue heating gently for a further 2 or 3 minutes. Season to taste with salt then serve immediately with tortilla chips, sliced vegetables, or flat breads.

nut and cream cheese peppers

THESE ARE TASTY AND ATTRACTIVE APPETIZERS. **SERVES 4**

**1 cup mixed shelled unsalted nuts
(peanuts, cashews, almonds, etc.)**

Salt

Cayenne pepper

1 cup low-fat cream cheese

1 clove garlic, crushed

Freshly ground black pepper

1 medium red bell pepper

1 medium green bell pepper

Whole-wheat toast

1 Heat a nonstick skillet over medium heat until hot, then add the nuts and cook until browned on all sides. Scatter salt and cayenne over some kitchen towels, add the hot nuts, and toss in the seasonings. Chop the nuts roughly when cooled.

2 Beat the cream cheese until smooth, then add the garlic and nuts. Season to taste with extra salt, if necessary, and black pepper. Cut the tops from the peppers and remove the seeds and cores. Pack the filling into the peppers, pressing it down firmly with the back of a spoon.

3 Chill the peppers for 2 to 3 hours before slicing crosswise in 4. Serve one slice of each pepper to each person, with whole-wheat toast.

roasted tomato tartlets

FOR AN EXTRA MEDITERRANEAN TASTE ADD A FEW OLIVES TO THE FILLING. **SERVES 6**

DOUGH

1½ cups (375 mL) fine whole-wheat flour

¼ cup (60 mL) sesame seeds

½ tsp (2 mL) salt

1 large egg, beaten

⅓ cup (90 mL) olive oil

3 to 4 Tbsp (45 to 50 mL) water

3 small onions, finely sliced

2 small cloves garlic, halved

3 Tbsp (45 mL) fruity olive oil

3 to 4 sprigs fresh thyme

2 bay leaves

4 to 5 large tomatoes, sliced

Salt and freshly ground black pepper

1 Mix together the flour, sesame seeds, and salt, then make a well in the center. Add the egg and olive oil and mix to a soft dough, adding water as necessary. Divide the mixture into 6 and shape to line six 4-in (10-cm) individual tart tins – this dough is easiest to mold into shape with your fingers. Chill the tart shells for at least 30 minutes while preparing the filling.

2 Cook the onions and garlic in the olive oil with the thyme sprigs and bay leaves for 30 to 40 minutes, until well-softened and reduced. Season to taste with salt and pepper, then remove the herbs.

3 Preheat the oven to 425°F (220°C). Fill the tart shells with the onion mixture, then top with the tomatoes, overlapping the slices and brushing them lightly with olive oil. Season well with salt and pepper and bake in the preheated oven for 20 to 25 minutes, until the dough is crisp and the tomatoes are just starting to blacken. Serve hot or cold with a salad of small greens.

quick-bake calabrian pizzas

FULL OF SOUTHERN ITALIAN FLAVORS, THESE PIZZAS ARE STRONG, PUNGENT, AND EXCITING. **SERVES 6**

DOUGH

2 cups (500 mL) whole-wheat flour

1 tsp (5 mL) salt

1 package active dry yeast

1 Tbsp (15 mL) olive oil

¾ cup (175 mL) warm water

6 tsp (30 mL) tapenade

1 red onion, finely sliced

12 halves sun-dried tomatoes in oil, chopped

1 Tbsp (15 mL) basil leaves, roughly torn

Salt and freshly ground black pepper

2-oz (60-g) can anchovy fillets, chopped

4 oz (125 g) mozzarella cheese, sliced

1 Mix together the flour, salt, and yeast in a bowl and make a well in the center. Add the oil and most of the water, then mix to a soft but manageable dough, adding more water if necessary. Knead well until smooth and elastic.

2 Preheat the oven to 425°F (220°C). Divide the dough into 6 parts and roll out into circles 6 in (15 cm) in diameter. Fold the edges of the dough over to form a lip, then place the bases on lightly greased baking sheets. Cover and leave in a warm place for 20 to 25 minutes, until the dough rises.

3 Spread each pizza base with 1 tsp (5 mL) of tapenade, arrange the onion over the bases and scatter with the chopped sun-dried tomatoes. Add the torn basil leaves with plenty of salt and pepper, and scatter the chopped anchovies over the pizzas. Arrange the mozzarella slices over the pizzas, then spoon the oil from the anchovies over the cheese.

4 Bake the pizzas in the preheated oven for 15 minutes, until the bases are crisp and the cheese has melted. Serve immediately.

88   **ABOVE** RATATOUILLE WITH MELON

spiced vegetables with yogurt

THIS DISH CAN BE SERVED COLD, BUT I MUCH PREFER IT WARM. **SERVES 6**

1¼ lb (600 g) prepared vegetables (zucchini, eggplant, bell pepper, cucumber, onions, mushrooms, etc.) sliced or julienned

2 plump cloves garlic, crushed

1 tsp (5 mL) cumin seeds

1 Tbsp (15 mL) coriander seeds

3 green cardamoms, crushed and seeded

3 Tbsp (45 mL) oil

¾ cup (175 mL) chickpeas, freshly cooked or canned, drained

1 cup (250 mL) thick plain yogurt

Grated rind of 1 lemon

2 Tbsp (25 mL) chopped cilantro

Salt and freshly ground black pepper

1 Tbsp (15 mL) finely grated fresh ginger

1 Prepare the vegetables and mix with the crushed garlic. Heat a nonstick skillet and add the cumin, coriander, and cardamom seeds. Fry gently for 1 to 2 minutes until the seeds begin to pop, then transfer the spices to a mortar and pestle or a spice mill and grind – the ground spices may be sifted to remove excess coriander husks, if preferred.

2 Heat the oil in the spice pan, add the vegetables, and cook for 4 to 5 minutes, until they begin to soften. Return the spices to the pan, add the chickpeas, and continue cooking until the vegetables are tender and the beans are hot.

3 Mix the yogurt with the lemon rind and chopped cilantro, then pour it over the vegetables in the pan. Mix gently, then add salt and pepper to taste before adding the grated ginger. Serve immediately, or let cool first.

ratatouille with melon

WATERMELON IS A GREAT ALTERNATIVE MELON FOR THIS DISH. **SERVES 8**

1 large onion, sliced

1 medium eggplant, sliced

4 Tbsp (50 mL) olive oil

2 medium zucchini, thickly sliced

1 medium green bell pepper, diced

2 to 3 plump cloves garlic, finely sliced

Two 14-fl oz (398-mL) cans chopped tomatoes

Salt and freshly ground black pepper

2 to 3 Tbsp (15 to 25 mL) freshly torn basil leaves

2 to 3 cups (500 to 750 mL) melon balls, either honeydew, cantaloupe, or watermelon

1 Cook the onion and eggplant in the olive oil until the eggplant starts to brown, then add the zucchini, bell pepper, and garlic and cook for a further 5 minutes. Add the chopped tomatoes, salt, and pepper and bring to a boil. Simmer for about 10 minutes, until the sauce has thickened but the vegetables still retain their texture.

2 Season the ratatouille to taste, then leave to cool. Add the basil and melon just before serving at room temperature.

(If you are preparing this dish to use in the recipe Ratatouille and Goat Cheese Quiche, see page 111, do not add melon.)

eggplant pâté

THIS PÂTÉ OOZES MEDITERRANEAN PROMISE AND CAN DOUBLE AS A DIP. **SERVES 6 TO 8**

1 small onion, finely chopped

1 Tbsp (15 mL) olive oil

1 medium eggplant, trimmed and thinly sliced

1 small clove garlic, crushed

½ cup (125 mL) tomato purée or thick tomato juice

1 Tbsp (15 mL) fresh oregano

1 cup (250 mL) low-fat cream cheese

Salt and freshly ground black pepper

1 Cook the onion in the oil until it starts to soften, then add the eggplant slices and cook, covered, for about 10 minutes until tender. Add the garlic and allow to cool.

2 Blend the eggplant mixture with all the remaining ingredients in a blender or food processor until almost smooth – the eggplant skin will keep the texture of the pâté slightly grainy. Season to taste, then chill for 30 minutes. The pâté should not be served too cold as this will impair the flavor – if it has been chilled overnight it should be allowed to stand at room temperature for about an hour before serving.

hummus

THIS MIDDLE EASTERN DIP IS DELICIOUS WITH FRESH BREAD OR CRUDITÉS. **SERVES 8**

1 cup (250 mL) chickpeas, soaked overnight or canned

2 to 3 plump cloves garlic

½ cup (125 mL) tahini

⅓ cup (90 mL) olive oil

Salt and freshly ground black pepper

Juice of ½ lemon (optional)

Paprika

1 Rinse the chickpeas under cold running water, and bring them to boil in a pot of fresh water and simmer for about 1½ hours, until tender. Leave to cool, then drain the beans, reserving some of the water. If using canned, drain and reserve the liquid.

2 Place the chickpeas in a blender or food processor with the garlic, tahini, and olive oil and blend until smooth. Add as much water from the beans as necessary to make a thick paste – about ⅔ cup (150 mL). Season well with salt and pepper, then add lemon juice to taste.

3 Spoon the hummus into a serving dish and chill lightly. Sprinkle with paprika just before serving with warm whole-wheat pita bread.

deviled leek crostini

SERVE WITH CRISP SALAD OR SOUP. **SERVES 4**

4 slices whole-wheat bread

2 small leeks, finely sliced

2 plump cloves garlic, crushed

3 Tbsp (45 mL) fruity olive oil

**1 tsp (5 mL) dry mustard, or
2 tsp (10 mL) mustard**

1 tsp (5 mL) cayenne pepper

**⅔ cup (150 mL) freshly grated
Parmesan cheese**

3 Tbsp (45 mL) sour cream

1 Preheat the oven to 350°F (175°C). Bake the bread on a baking sheet for 25 to 30 minutes, until dry and crisp. For extra flavor, the bread may be brushed lightly with olive oil before baking.

2 Cook the leeks and garlic in the oil until they begin to soften, then add the mustard and cayenne. Continue cooking until the leeks are very soft. Add the cheese and cream, then season well with salt, pepper, and extra cayenne as required.

3 Spread the leeks over the prepared toasts and cook under a hot broiler for 2 to 3 minutes, until the leeks start to brown. Serve immediately.

ABOVE GUACAMOLE

stuffed anaheim chiles

DON'T PEEL THE CHILES – THE SKIN WILL COME OFF EASILY WHEN THEY ARE COOKED. **SERVES 4**

1 small onion, finely chopped

1 Tbsp (15 mL) oil

1 tsp (5 mL) ground allspice

½ tsp (2 mL) chili powder

½ cup (125 mL) red lentils

14-fl oz (398-mL) can chopped tomatoes

¾ cup (175 mL) water or stock

½ tsp (2 mL) salt

4 large Anaheim chiles

¾ cup (175 mL) soft goat cheese

1 Cook the onion in the oil until softened but not browned, then add the spices and cook slowly for another minute. Stir in the lentils, tomatoes, and water and season with the salt. Bring to a boil and simmer for about 30 minutes, until the lentils are soft. Season to taste, adding extra salt if necessary.

2 Preheat the oven to 400°F (200°C). Cut the chiles in half lengthwise and remove the membranes and seeds. Place the shells in a roasting pan, then fill them with the lentil mixture and top with spoonfuls of the goat cheese.

3 Bake the chiles in the preheated oven for 30 minutes until the cheese has melted and browned and the chiles are tender. Serve immediately.

guacamole

A TRUE GUACAMOLE SHOULD HAVE A SLIGHTLY ROUGH TEXTURE, NOT BE BLENDED TO A PASTE. **SERVES 4**

2 large ripe avocados

2 medium tomatoes, seeded and chopped

1 small mild green chile, seeded and finely chopped

Grated rind and juice of 1 lime

2 scallions, trimmed and finely chopped

1 to 2 medium cloves garlic, crushed

½ tsp (2 mL) salt

1 Scoop the flesh from the avocados and mash it roughly with a fork. Add all the remaining ingredients, seasoning gradually with the salt to taste.

2 Serve at room temperature or chilled with corn chips, tortilla chips, or sliced vegetables.

stuffed zucchini with tomato sauce

BOAT-SHAPED ZUCCHINI ARE PERFECT FOR HOLDING STUFFINGS. **SERVES 4**

- **4 small zucchini, trimmed**
- **1 large onion, finely chopped**
- **1 cup (250 mL) roughly chopped button mushrooms**
- **2 small cloves garlic**
- **2 Tbsp (25 mL) oil**
- **½ cup (125 mL) fresh whole-wheat bread crumbs**
- **Salt and freshly ground black pepper**
- **1 Tbsp (15 mL) pine nuts**
- **1 Tbsp (15 mL) sunflower seeds**
- **1 Tbsp (15 mL) basil leaves, roughly torn**
- **14-fl oz (398-mL) can chopped tomatoes**
- **½ cup (125 mL) grated Cheddar cheese (optional)**

1 Preheat the oven to 375°F (190°C). Cut each zucchini in half lengthwise and scoop out the flesh with a teaspoon. Arrange the shells in a buttered ovenproof dish, chop the reserved flesh, and set to one side.

2 Finely chop half the onion, the mushrooms, and 1 clove garlic in a food processor. Cook the mixture in 1 Tbsp (15 mL) of oil until the juices run from the mushrooms, then remove from the heat and mix in the bread crumbs, seasonings, and zucchini flesh. Add the pine nuts and sunflower seeds, then stuff the mixture into the zucchini shells, and pack well.

3 Prepare the tomato sauce by cooking the remaining onion in the remaining oil until soft. Crush the remaining garlic and add it with the basil and tomatoes. Season well, then simmer for about 10 minutes, until reduced and thickened. Pour the sauce over the zucchini, sprinkle with the grated cheese if used, and bake in the preheated oven for 20 to 25 minutes, until the zucchini is tender. Serve with a salad.

crab with ginger and grapefruit

I FIRST HAD THIS DISH IN A RESTAURANT IN SELSEY, ONE OF THE BEST CRAB-PRODUCING AREAS IN ENGLAND. THIS IS WORTH SPENDING ON FRESH CRABS. **SERVES 2**

- **2 dressed crabs or 4-oz (125 g) crab meat**
- **½ cup (125 mL) fresh brown bread crumbs**
- **1 medium grapefruit**
- **Salt and freshly ground black pepper**
- **1-in (2.5-cm) piece ginger, grated**

1 Scoop the crab meat from the shells into a bowl and set the shells aside. Mix the crab meat with the bread crumbs. Grate the rind from the grapefruit, then add it to the crab with the chopped flesh of the fruit. Season well, add the ginger. Arrange the mixture in the shells and carefully clean the edges.

2 Preheat the broiler, then broil the crabs under medium heat for 5 to 6 minutes until piping hot. Serve just as they are, or with a very small salad garnish.

crab balls with sweet lime sauce

USE TINNED OR FRESH CRABMEAT, WHICHEVER IS EASIEST. **SERVES 4**

SAUCE

Grated rind and juice of 2 limes

1 Tbsp (15 mL) Demerara sugar

1 small red chile, seeded and very finely chopped

8-oz (250-g) can white crab meat, drained and squeezed dry

1 cup (250 mL) fresh whole-wheat bread crumbs

4 scallions, trimmed and very finely chopped

Salt and freshly ground black pepper

Nutmeg

1 large egg, beaten

⅓ cup (90 mL) sunflower oil

1 Mix all the ingredients for the sauce together and set aside until needed.

2 Mix the crab meat with the bread crumbs and scallions then season with salt, pepper, and nutmeg. Add the egg and blend the mixture together. Shape into 20 walnut-sized pieces – you may have to flour your hands to do this.

3 Heat the oil in a skillet and add the crab balls. Fry them for 4 to 5 minutes until evenly browned all over, turning occasionally. Drain on paper towels, then serve immediately with the lime sauce for dipping.

3 Main dishes

A high-fiber diet based on grains and legumes may appear to be little different from a vegetarian eating pattern but not all high-fiber disciples have forsaken meat. I am a meat eater but, like so many other people, I now eat significantly less meat than I used to. By following a high-fiber diet and incorporating recipes that not only taste good but are also varied in style and texture, and filling, I do not miss the meat that I used to eat.

Several of the dishes included here contain a mixture of meat or poultry and high-fiber foods. For example, in place of the classic Beef Bourguignon, which is often rich and heavy, I have included a Chicken and Lima Bean Bourguignon. The chicken contains less fat than beef and the beans mean that you need less chicken in each helping, creating a very healthy alternative to the classic beef recipe.

Some of these dishes contain pasta and it makes sense to use a whole-wheat variety in a high-fiber diet. I have yet to find an acceptable commercial whole-wheat pasta, so I have made my own pasta for these recipes. Providing that you use a fine whole-wheat flour, the pasta is easy to make, but a bread flour will be too coarse and the bran will tear the dough. As none of the recipes rely on the pasta for all their fiber, a regular white pasta will not diminish the fiber content of the dish.

I have not included any recipes for baked potatoes in this book, but they are certainly a very useful high-fiber food. If you feel your main dish is short of the essential ingredient, then serve a baked potato with it and eat it with the skin. However, a baked potato without butter or sour cream is like a tomato without salt, so watch the calories.

LEFT APPLE RATATOUILLE WITH SPICED PORK (SEE PAGE 142)

corn mexicali

YOU WILL NEED A STRONG, SHARP KNIFE TO CUT THROUGH THE CORN. **SERVES 4**

4 large ears of corn, husked

4 Tbsp (50 mL) oil

1 medium onion, finely chopped

1 tsp (5 mL) mild chile powder

1 tsp (5 mL) ground cumin

1 plump clove garlic, crushed

1 small green bell pepper, seeded and chopped

Two 14-fl oz (398-mL) cans chopped tomatoes

Salt and freshly ground black pepper

2 Tbsp (25 mL) chopped fresh cilantro

Tortillas or corn chips

1 Cut the corn cobs into slices approximately 1 in (2.5 cm) thick. Heat 2 Tbsp (25 mL) of oil in a large skillet, add the corn slices, and cook quickly on both sides until they start to brown. Remove from the pan with a slotted spoon.

2 Heat the remaining oil in the skillet; add the onion and cook until it starts to brown. Add the spices and cook for another minute over low heat. Stir in the garlic, pepper, and tomatoes and bring to a boil. Return the corn to the pan and simmer 30 minutes, turning the slices once.

3 Transfer the corn slices to a warmed serving dish. Cook the sauce to reduce and thicken, then season to taste. Add the cilantro; pour the sauce over the corn and serve immediately with tortillas, Mexican rice, refried beans, or corn chips.

chickpeas with sesame sauce

A STRONGLY AND UNUSUALLY FLAVORED VEGETARIAN DISH, IDEAL FOR THE EXOTICALLY MINDED. **SERVES 4**

2 large onions, finely sliced

2 Tbsp (25 mL) fruity olive oil

2 tsp (10 mL) ground cumin

1 tsp (5 mL) ground allspice

1 red chile, seeded and sliced

4 large cloves garlic, finely sliced

1½ cups (375 mL) chickpeas, soaked overnight, or canned

14-fl oz (398-mL) can chopped tomatoes

1 cup (250 mL) dry white wine

1½ cups (375 mL) rich vegetable stock

Salt and freshly ground black pepper

¼ cup (60 mL) sesame seeds, toasted

1 Tbsp (15 mL) tahini

1 Preheat the oven to 325°F (160°C). Cook the onions in the olive oil in a flameproof casserole dish until soft but not browned, add the cumin, allspice, chile, and garlic and continue cooking over low heat for 1 or 2 minutes. Drain and rinse the chickpeas under cold running water, then add them to the pot with the tomatoes, white wine, and enough stock to just cover the chickpeas. Season well with salt and pepper, cover and cook in the preheated oven for 1½ hours.

2 Stir the toasted sesame seeds and tahini into the casserole and season to taste. Garnish with mint and lemon rind, if you like, before serving.

lentil and pumpkin lasagne

PUMPKIN AND LENTILS MAKE A SATISFYING ALTERNATIVE TO THE TRADITIONAL MEAT
FILLING FOR LASAGNE. **SERVES 6**

1 large onion, finely chopped

2 Tbsp (25 mL) olive oil

1 medium zucchini, diced

**1 medium green bell pepper, seeded
and diced**

1 to 2 medium cloves garlic, crushed

**1 lb (450 g) pumpkin purée, fresh or
canned**

¾ cup (175 mL) red lentils

**14-fl oz (398-mL) can chopped
tomatoes**

3 cups (750 mL) rich vegetable stock

Salt and freshly ground black pepper

**2 Tbsp (25 mL) chopped fresh mixed
herbs**

**Fresh whole-wheat lasagne made with
1 cup (250 mL) whole-wheat flour
and 1 large egg or 6 large whole-
wheat lasagne noodles**

1½ cups (375 mL) ricotta cheese

1½ cups (375 mL) sour cream

**1 cup (125 mL) grated Cheddar
cheese, loosely packed**

1 Cook the onion in the oil until softened but not browned,
then stir in the zucchini and pepper and cook for another
2 minutes. Add the garlic, pumpkin purée, lentils, and
tomatoes and stir well. Add the stock, herbs, and seasonings
and bring the sauce to a boil. Simmer for 20 to 25 minutes,
until the lentils are soft and the sauce has thickened.

2 Preheat the oven to 400°F (200°C). Prepare the pasta by
mixing together the flour and egg, then process it
through a pasta machine into 6 thin strips of lasagne. Bring a
large pot of water to a boil and cook the lasagne quickly, 2 or
3 sheets at a time, for 1 to 2 minutes, until it floats to the top
of the pot. Drain and set aside.

3 Place half the lentil mixture in the bottom of a suitable
buttered ovenproof dish and top with half the pasta.
Repeat the layers. Mix the ricotta and sour cream together and
season with salt and pepper. Add half the cheese, spread the
mixture over the lasagne and top with the remaining cheese.

4 Bake the lasagne in the preheated oven for 30 to
40 minutes, until the topping is set and brown.

vegetable tortillas with mixed bean salsa

DON'T OVERFILL THE TORTILLAS – THEY ARE BEST EATEN WITH YOUR FINGERS. **SERVES 4**

SALSA

15-oz (425-g) can mixed beans, drained and rinsed

1 small red onion, finely chopped

2 small cloves garlic, finely chopped

⅓ cup (90 mL) diced cucumber

1 red chile, seeded and finely chopped

1 medium avocado, chopped

1 Tbsp (15 mL) orange juice

1 Tbsp (15 mL) white wine vinegar

Salt and freshly ground black pepper

2 Tbsp (25 mL) olive oil

1¼ lb (600 g) diced mixed vegetables (leeks, onions, celery, mushrooms, bell peppers, etc.)

1 tsp (5 mL) chili powder

14-fl oz (398-mL) can chopped tomatoes

Salt and freshly ground black pepper

TO SERVE

12 flour tortillas, warmed

Grated Cheddar cheese

Sour cream

Chopped cilantro to serve

1 Prepare the salsa by mixing all the ingredients together and leaving for up to 1 hour, to allow the flavors to blend.

2 Heat the oil in a large skillet or wok; add all the prepared vegetables and stir-fry quickly for 2 to 3 minutes. Stir in the chili powder and the tomatoes and cook for a further 5 minutes, until the vegetables are just softened. Season to taste.

3 Spread some of the vegetable mixture over a tortilla, then top it with grated cheese. Add some salsa and sour cream. Dust with chili powder and sprinkle with cilantro. Then roll up and eat.

brazil nut loaf

THIS MOIST, SPICY LOAF IS COMPLEMENTED NICELY BY TANGY SALSA. **SERVES 6**

1 large onion

8 oz (225 g) mushrooms

2 plump cloves garlic

1 Tbsp (15 mL) ground coriander

1 tsp (5 mL) ground ginger

2 Tbsp (25 mL) oil

7-oz (200-g) can chopped tomatoes

1 Tbsp (15 mL) tomato paste

1½ cups (375 mL) brazil nuts, roughly chopped

1 cup (250 mL) fresh whole-wheat bread crumbs

Salt and freshly ground black pepper

1 large egg, beaten

SALSA

1 Tbsp (15 mL) cumin seeds

½ cucumber, diced

2 medium tomatoes, diced

1 small mild red chile, seeded and diced

4 scallions, trimmed and finely sliced

2 large cloves garlic, finely chopped

Salt and freshly ground black pepper

2 Tbsp (25 mL) white wine vinegar

1 Preheat the oven to 375°F (190°C) and lightly grease a large loaf pot. Chop the onion in a food processor; add the mushrooms and garlic and process until the whole mixture is a thick paste. Cook the paste with the spices in the oil for 4 to 5 minutes, until the juices run from the mushrooms. Add the canned tomatoes and tomato paste and cook for a further 4 to 5 minutes, to reduce the tomato juice.

2 Transfer the mixture to a large bowl and add the chopped nuts and bread crumbs. Season well with salt and pepper, then bind with the beaten egg. Spoon the mixture into the prepared pot, cover with lightly oiled foil, and bake in the preheated oven for 1 hour, or until set. Remove the foil and cook for a further 10 to 15 minutes.

3 Meanwhile, prepare the salsa. Heat a nonstick skillet, add the cumin seeds, and roast for 1 to 2 minutes. Crush lightly in a mortar and pestle. Combine the cumin with the remaining ingredients and leave the salsa for about 1 hour. Stir before serving.

hazelnut and zucchini pasta

WHOLE-WHEAT PASTA IS EASY TO MAKE IF YOU USE FINE WHOLE-WHEAT FLOUR – OR USE
PREPARED PASTA IF YOU PREFER. **SERVES 4**

2 Tbsp (25 mL) butter

2 to 3 Tbsp (15 to 25 mL) olive oil

**4 to 6 small green and yellow
zucchini, sliced diagonally**

2 to 3 plump cloves garlic, crushed

**½ cup (125 mL) hazelnuts, toasted
and roughly chopped**

**½ cup (125 mL) freshly grated
Parmesan cheese**

Salt and freshly ground black pepper

PASTA

12 oz (350 g) whole-wheat flour

2 medium eggs

**or use prepared whole-wheat
tagliatelle or fettucine**

1 Heat the butter and oil together; add the zucchini slices and cook over medium-high heat until browned and softened. This takes about 12 to 15 minutes. Add the garlic and hazelnuts to the pan once the zucchini have started to soften.

2 Mix the flour with the eggs to make a firm pasta dough. Knead thoroughly, then process through a pasta machine and cut into tagliatelle. Bring a large pot of salted water to a boil; add the pasta and boil quickly for 2 to 3 minutes, until just tender. If using prepared pasta, cook as instructed on the package.

3 Drain the pasta, shake briefly, then add to the zucchini mixture in the pan. Toss well, seasoning with salt and pepper, then sprinkle over the Parmesan, which will melt over the hot pasta. Serve immediately, while still hot.

pasta primavera

A CELEBRATION OF THE FIRST MONTHS OF SUMMER WITH ITS SMALL, BRIGHT GREEN, FULL-FLAVORED VEGETABLES. **SERVES 4**

1 cup (250 mL) sugar or snow peas, trimmed

1 cup (250 mL) green beans, trimmed and halved

1½ cups (375 mL) trimmed and chopped asparagus

1 cup (250 mL) shelled fava beans

1 small leek, trimmed and finely sliced

1 Tbsp (15 mL) butter

1 cup (250 mL) heavy cream

1 to 2 Tbsp (15 to 25 mL) chopped fresh parsley

2 cups (500 mL) whole-wheat pasta

1 Bring a large pot of salted water to a boil. Cook the peas, beans, and asparagus individually, plunging them into iced water immediately to prevent overcooking. Cook the peas for 2 minutes; green beans for 1 minute; asparagus stalks for 3 minutes, then add the asparagus tips and cook for a further 2 minutes; and the fava beans for 3 minutes.

2 In a large pot, cook the leek slowly in the butter until soft but not brown, then add the cream and heat until almost boiling. Drain the vegetables and add them to the pot, then heat gently for 2 to 3 minutes until piping hot. Stir in the parsley.

3 Cook the pasta in a large pot of boiling salted water, drain and shake dry. Add the pasta to the vegetables, tossing it in the cream, and serve immediately.

spinach and walnut whole-wheat quiche

WALNUTS GIVE A DELICIOUS CRUNCH TO THIS QUICHE. **SERVES 4 TO 6**

PASTRY

½ cup (125 mL) butter

1¼ cups (310 mL) whole-wheat flour

Pinch of salt

FILLING

1 lb (450 g) frozen or fresh chopped spinach

Salt and freshly ground black pepper

Nutmeg

⅔ cup (150 mL) walnut pieces, chopped

½ cup (125 mL) blue cheese, crumbled (Stilton or Danish)

1¼ cups (300 mL) milk

2 large eggs

1 Preheat the oven to 400°F (200°C). Blend the butter with the flour and salt in a bowl until the mixture resembles fine bread crumbs. Mix to a manageable dough with warm water, then roll out and use the pastry to line a 9-in (23-cm) loose-bottomed pie pan. Line with paper towels then fill with dry beans. Bake in the preheated oven for 20 minutes.

2 Cook the spinach gently in a covered pot until piping hot; shake from time to time to prevent it from burning. Squeeze the spinach dry, then season to taste with salt, pepper, and nutmeg.

3 Remove the paper and beans from the pastry and fill with a layer of the spinach, then a layer of walnuts. Crumble the blue cheese over the top of the filling.

4 Beat the milk and eggs and season with salt and pepper. Pour the custard over the spinach filling, then sprinkle with nutmeg. Reduce the oven temperature to 375°F (190°C) and bake the quiche for 25 to 30 minutes, until set. Serve warm or cold.

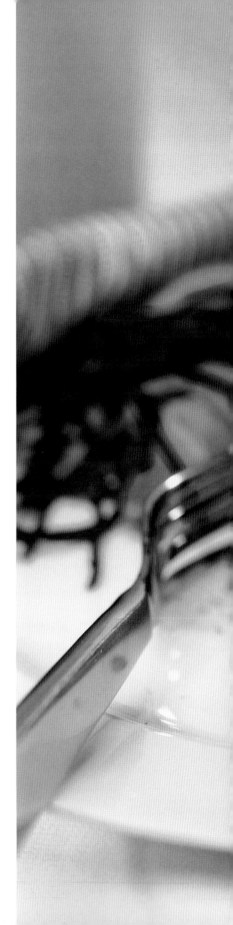

ABOVE RATATOUILLE & GOAT CHEESE QUICHE

ratatouille and goat cheese quiche

I SOMETIMES ADD NUTS TO THE VEGETABLES TO GIVE EXTRA TEXTURE. **SERVES 4 TO 6**

PASTRY

⅔ cup (150 mL) butter

¾ cup (175 mL) whole-wheat flour

Pinch of salt

1¾ cup (425 mL) ratatouille
(see p. 89)

1 Tbsp (15 mL) basil leaves, roughly
torn

⅔ cup (150 mL) soft goat cheese

Salt and freshly ground black pepper

1¼ cups (300 mL) milk or milk and
light cream, mixed

2 large eggs, beaten

1 Preheat the oven to 400°F (200°C). Prepare the pastry by blending the butter into the flour and salt until the mixture resembles fine bread crumbs. Mix to a firm, manageable dough with warm water, then knead lightly on a floured surface and roll out to line a deep 7-in (18-cm) pie pan. Chill the pastry lightly for 10 to 15 minutes, then line the pastry case with paper towels and fill with dry beans. Bake for 15 minutes in the preheated oven.

2 Remove the paper and the beans and spread the ratatouille over the partly cooked pastry. Sprinkle the basil leaves and goat cheese over and season with pepper. Beat together the milk, the eggs, and some seasoning, then pour the mixture into the pastry over the vegetables and cheese. Return the quiche to the oven, reduce the heat to 375°F (190°C) and cook for a further 35 minutes or until set. This quiche is best served warm.

millet and vegetable gratin

THIS RICH GRATIN IS PERFECT FOR A WINTER'S EVENING. **SERVES 6**

2 cups (500 mL) millet, washed

1 large carrot, finely sliced

1 medium onion, finely sliced

8 strips bacon, finely chopped

2 cups (500 mL) sliced button
mushrooms

2 cups (500 mL) thick tomato juice

Salt and freshly ground black pepper

2 Tbsp (25 mL) basil leaves, roughly
torn

½ cup (125 mL) grated Cheddar
cheese

1 Preheat the oven to 375°F (190°C). Add the millet to a large pot of boiling water and simmer for 20 minutes, then drain. Cook the carrot and the onion with the bacon until they start to soften, then add the sliced mushrooms. Cook for a further 5 minutes until all the vegetables are soft.

2 Add the tomato juice and the drained millet, season well with salt and pepper and add the basil. Transfer to a buttered, ovenproof dish and bake in the preheated oven for 40 minutes. Scatter the cheese over the millet and return the dish to the oven for a further 30 minutes. Serve hot with a spicy tomato sauce or chutney.

curried lentil soufflé

LENTILS ARE AN UNUSUAL BASE FOR A SOUFFLÉ, AND CURRY AN UNUSUAL FLAVORING, BUT THE FINISHED DISH IS DELICIOUS. **SERVES 3**

⅔ cup (150 mL) red lentils

1 to 2 tsp (15 to 25 mL) curry powder

1½ cups (375 mL) stock or water

2 Tbsp (25 mL) butter

1 Tbsp (15 mL) whole-wheat flour

⅔ cup (150 mL) milk

1 Tbsp (15 mL) Dijon mustard

3 large eggs, separated

Salt and freshly ground black pepper

1 Preheat the oven to 350°F (175°C) and lightly grease a 6-in (15-cm) soufflé dish. Bring the lentils, curry powder, and water to a boil in a pot, and simmer for 10 to 15 minutes until the lentils have softened and cooked to a thick purée. Beat smooth, then transfer to a bowl to cool slightly.

2 Melt the butter in the same pot and stir in the flour. Cook slowly for 1 minute, then gradually add the milk. Bring to a boil, stirring all the time and cook until very thick. Add the mustard, egg yolks, and lentils and blend well. Season lightly.

3 Whisk the egg whites until stiff, then fold them into the lentil mixture. Turn into the prepared dish. Bake in the preheated oven for 30 to 40 minutes, until set. Serve immediately.

bean and vegetable turnovers

A TASTY VEGETARIAN ALTERNATIVE TO THE FAMOUS PIES FROM CORNWALL, SOUTHWEST ENGLAND. **SERVES 4**

⅓ cup (90 mL) mung beans, soaked
    overnight

PASTRY

½ cup (125 mL) butter

1 cup (250 mL) whole-wheat flour

Pinch of salt

1 medium onion, finely chopped

¾ cup (175 mL) finely diced mixed
    root vegetables

½ cup (125 mL) grated or finely diced
    Cheddar cheese

Salt and freshly ground black pepper

1 Tbsp chopped fresh mixed herbs
    (optional)

1 Drain the beans and rinse them thoroughly under cold running water. Bring to a boil in a pot of fresh water, simmer for 30 minutes until tender. Drain and set aside.

2 Preheat the oven to 400°F (200°C). Prepare the pastry by blending the butter into the flour and salt. Add warm water to give a firm but workable dough, then knead lightly on a floured surface. Divide the dough into 4 and roll out into 6-in (15-cm) diameter circles – cut around a small plate.

3 Mix the mung beans with the remaining ingredients and divide the mixture among the pastry circles. Dampen the edges with water, then draw the pastry together over the filling, pinching the edges together to seal them. Place the turnovers on a lightly oiled baking sheet. Cook in the preheated oven for 30 to 35 minutes, until the pastry is crisp. Serve hot or cold.

quick bean pot

CANNED BEANS TAKE HOURS OFF THE PREPARATION WITH NO LOSS OF FLAVOR! **SERVES 6**

1 large onion, finely sliced

2 Tbsp (25 mL) olive oil

1 cup (250 mL) sliced carrots

1 cup (250 mL) turnip, finely diced

2 cups (500 mL) zucchini, sliced

Two 15-oz (425-g) cans beans with their juice, e.g. mixed beans and red kidney beans

2 Tbsp (25 mL) fresh oregano, chopped

Salt and freshly ground black pepper

2 Tbsp (25 mL) tomato paste

⅔ cup (150 mL) grated Cheddar cheese

1 Cook the onion in the oil in a large flameproof casserole dish until softened but not browned, then add the carrot and turnip and cook for 3 to 4 minutes. Stir in the zucchini, beans and juice, the herbs, the seasonings, and the tomato paste. Bring to a boil, then simmer for 30 to 40 minutes, until the vegetables are tender and the broth is reduced to below the level of the beans.

2 Preheat the broiler. Season the casserole to taste and sprinkle with the cheese. Cook under the broiler until the cheese has melted and browned.

spinach and pancetta risotto

FOR A PERFECT RISOTTO, ALLOW THE STOCK TO BE ABSORBED AT EACH STEP. **SERVES 4**

1 large onion, finely sliced

3 Tbsp (45 mL) olive oil

2 cloves garlic, crushed

1½ cups (375 mL) arborio rice

5 cups (1.25 L) rich vegetable stock

5 slices pancetta or thick bacon

Salt and freshly ground black pepper

Nutmeg

6 cups (1.5 L) spinach, shredded
  coarsely

Parmesan cheese shavings to serve

1 Cook the onion in the oil until softened but not brown, then add the garlic and rice and cook over a low heat for a further 1 minute. Add one-third of the stock, then stir gently until it has been absorbed, then add half the remainder and simmer again. Stir-fry the pancetta in a dry non-stick skillet until crispy and set aside.

2 Season the risotto well then add the spinach with the remaining stock and cook until the spinach has wilted and the stock has almost been absorbed. Serve the risotto garnished with the pancetta and slivers of Parmesan.

spiced baked beans

THIS IS MY VERSION OF THE FAMED BOSTON BAKED BEANS. **SERVES 4**

1½ cups (375 mL) black-eyed beans,
  soaked overnight, or canned

1 large onion, finely chopped

2 Tbsp (25 mL) oil

½ tsp (2 mL) chili powder

½ tsp (2 mL) ground cumin

1 to 2 plump cloves garlic, sliced

1 green chile, seeded and finely
  chopped

14-fl oz (398-mL) can chopped
  tomatoes

1 cup (250 mL) rich vegetable stock

Salt and freshly ground black pepper

1 thick pepperoni or garlic sausage,
  thickly sliced

1 Tbsp (15 mL) wine vinegar

½ to 1 Tbsp (7 to 15 mL) Demerara
  sugar

Chopped fresh parsley to garnish

1 Drain the beans and rinse thoroughly under cold running water; set aside. Cook the onion in the oil until soft, add the spices and cook slowly for another minute. Stir in the garlic, chile, and beans, then add the tomatoes and stock. Season lightly, bring to a boil, and cover to simmer for 45 minutes.

2 Season to taste with extra salt and pepper, then add the sliced sausage to the beans. Cover and simmer for a further 15 minutes. Season with the vinegar and sugar, stirring well, before garnishing with parsley.

ABOVE NAVY BEANS WITH BROCCOLI

navy beans with broccoli

THE SECRET OF A PERFECT CASSEROLE IS A WELL-FLAVORED STOCK. **SERVES 4**

1½ cups (375 mL) navy beans, soaked overnight, or canned

1 Tbsp (15 mL) oil

1 large onion, finely sliced

1 leek, trimmed and finely sliced

2 cups (500 mL) sliced button mushrooms

¼ tsp (2½ mL) mace

½ cup (125 mL) chopped fresh parsley

1 cup (250 mL) dry white wine

1 cup (250 mL) rich vegetable stock

Salt and freshly ground black pepper

½ small red bell pepper, finely chopped

1 cup (250 mL) small broccoli florets

2 Tbsp (25 mL) sour cream

1 Preheat the oven to 350°F (170°C). Drain the beans and rinse them well under cold running water.

2 Heat the oil in a flameproof casserole; add the onion and leek and cook until soft, then stir in the mushrooms and cook for a further 2 to 3 minutes until they soften. Add the beans, mace, half the parsley, white wine, and sufficient stock to just cover the beans. Season lightly with salt and pepper, then bring to a boil. Cover the casserole and cook in the preheated oven for 1½ hours, until the beans are tender.

3 Stir the beans; most of the liquid will have been absorbed but there should still be a little at the bottom of the pot. Add extra salt and pepper then stir in the red bell pepper and broccoli. Cover the pot and return it to the oven for a further 15 to 20 minutes until the broccoli is just tender. Stir in the sour cream and serve with steamed carrots or a tomato salad.

lentils and rice

THIS IS A FILLING DISH THAT CAN BE SERVED BY ITSELF OR WITH A GREEN SALAD. **SERVES 4 TO 6**

1½ cups (375 mL) brown rice

1 large onion, finely sliced

1 to 2 Tbsp (15 to 25 mL) curry powder, according to taste

3 Tbsp (45 mL) olive oil

1 cup (250 mL) cooked or canned lentils, drained

Salt and freshly ground black pepper

2 hard-boiled eggs, chopped

3 Tbsp (45 mL) heavy cream

1 to 2 Tbsp (15 to 25 mL) chopped fresh cilantro

1 Place the rice in a large pan of water; bring to a boil and simmer for 30 minutes, or until the rice is just tender. Drain.

2 Cook the onion with the curry powder in the oil over low heat until the onion is soft, then stir in the cooked rice and lentils. Cook for 2 to 3 minutes until piping hot, then add the chopped eggs and the cream, if used. Cook for a further 1 to 2 minutes.

3 Season well, then stir in the cilantro leaves and serve immediately.

curried vegetable casserole

A VEGETARIAN VERSION OF THE AFRICAN DISH, BOBOTIE. **SERVES 6**

2 medium onions, finely sliced

2 Tbsp (25 mL) sunflower oil

1 Tbsp (15 mL) medium curry powder

1 tsp (5 mL) turmeric

1½ lb (700 g) mixed diced root vegetables

2 Tbsp (25 mL) white wine vinegar

1 Tbsp (15 mL) dark brown sugar

1 tsp (5 mL) salt

½ tsp (2 mL) freshly ground black pepper

1 thick slice whole-wheat bread

⅔ cup (150 mL) seedless raisins

3 Tbsp (45 mL) fruit chutney

½ cup (125 mL) water

4 to 5 lime leaves (optional)

⅓ cup (90 mL) shredded almonds

1 large egg, beaten

⅔ cup (150 mL) milk

1 Preheat the oven to 350°F (175°C). Cook the onion in the oil until it begins to soften, then stir in the curry powder and the turmeric and cook for a further 1 to 2 minutes over low heat. Add the prepared root vegetables, vinegar, sugar, salt, and pepper and cook gently over low heat until the vegetables begin to soften.

2 Soak the bread in water for 3 to 4 minutes, then drain it, squeeze it dry, and add it to the vegetables. Stir in the raisins, chutney, and water, then pack the mixture into a buttered ovenproof dish. Bury the lime leaves in the mixture and cover the dish with buttered foil. Bake in the preheated oven for 1½ hours. Reduce the oven temperature to 300°F (150°C).

3 Remove the foil from the dish and sprinkle the almonds over the vegetables. Beat the egg with the milk, adding extra milk if necessary to make 1 cup (250 mL). Pour it over the vegetables; bake for a further 30 minutes at the lower temperature, until the custard has set. Serve with mango chutney and a mixed salad.

glamorgan sausages

THE ORIGINAL WELSH SAUSAGES WERE MADE WITH A LOCAL CHEESE, NOW NO LONGER AVAILABLE. **SERVES 4**

1 cup (250 mL) leeks, trimmed and finely sliced

1 Tbsp (15 mL) oil

1 cup (250 mL) cold mashed potato

1 cup (250 mL) grated old Cheddar cheese

Salt and freshly ground black pepper

1 tsp (5 mL) Dijon mustard

1 Tbsp (15 mL) freshly chopped parsley

1 cup (250 mL) fresh whole-wheat bread crumbs

2 to 3 Tbsp (25 to 45 mL) olive oil

1 Cook the leek in the oil until soft but not browned, then mix with all the remaining ingredients, except the oil, adding sufficient bread crumbs to make a very stiff dough. Divide into 8 then shape into sausages, flouring your hands to make it easy to handle the mixture.

2 Heat the oil in a skillet; add the sausages and cook quickly for 6 to 8 minutes, turning carefully to brown on all sides. Serve with a spicy fruit chutney or relish.

cracked wheat pilaf

VERY COARSE CRACKED WHEAT GIVES THE DISH A LIVELY, NUTTY TEXTURE. **SERVES 4**

1 large onion, sliced

1 medium leek, trimmed and sliced

2 Tbsp (25 mL) olive oil

1 tsp (5 mL) ground cumin

1 tsp (5 mL) ground ginger

1 to 2 plump cloves garlic, finely sliced

4 sticks celery, trimmed and sliced

1 medium red bell pepper, seeded and sliced

1 cup (250 mL) baby corn, halved

1½ cups (375 mL) cracked wheat

14-fl oz (398-mL) can chopped tomatoes

3 cups (750 mL) water or stock

Salt and freshly ground black pepper

1 cup (250 mL) snow peas, topped and tailed

6 halves sun-dried tomatoes, shredded

1 Cook the onion and leek in the oil until softened but not browned, then add the spices and cook for 1 minute. Add the garlic, celery, pepper, and corn, and cook briefly before stirring the cracked wheat into the pot.

2 Add the tomatoes, stock, and seasonings, then simmer for 12 to 15 minutes, stirring occasionally. Add the snow peas and sun-dried tomatoes and cook for a further 4 to 5 minutes. Serve with a tossed green salad.

millet rounds with yogurt sauce

MILLET REPLACES THE TRADITIONAL MEAT IN THIS VEGETARIAN ALTERNATIVE. **SERVES 4**

¾ cup (175 mL) raw millet

⅔ cup (150 mL) milk or milk and stock, mixed

1 Tbsp (15 mL) butter

1 heaping Tbsp (15 mL) whole-wheat flour

Salt and freshly ground black pepper

4 scallions, finely chopped

1 to 2 Tbsp (15 to 25 mL) freshly chopped dill

1½ cups (375 mL) fresh whole-wheat bread crumbs

YOGURT SAUCE

1 tsp (5 mL) cumin seeds

Grated rind and juice of 1 lemon

2 Tbsp (25 mL) chopped fresh cilantro

1½ cups (375 mL) plain yogurt

Salt and freshly ground black pepper

FOR FRYING

2 eggs, beaten

1 cup dried or toasted bread crumbs

⅓ cup (90 mL) oil

1 Add the millet to a large pot of boiling water and simmer for 20 minutes, until soft. Meanwhile, place the milk, butter, and flour in a pot and bring to a boil, stirring constantly. Simmer the sauce for 1 to 2 minutes until thickened, then season to taste and pour into a large bowl. Drain the millet and add it to the sauce with the scallions, dill, and bread crumbs. Mix together, and allow to cool.

2 Shape the mixture into 12 rounds or turnovers; coat your hands in flour and toss the rounds in the beaten eggs, then coat in the bread crumbs. Repeat this process if necessary to get a good coating.

3 Prepare the yogurt sauce. Toast the cumin seeds in a heavy-based skillet for 1 to 2 minutes, then crush lightly in a mortar and pestle or with the end of a rolling pin. Mix the cumin with the other sauce ingredients and place in a small pot over a very low heat to warm gently.

4 Heat the oil in the heavy skillet until hot, then add the rounds and cook for 10 to 12 minutes until well-browned. Serve with the yogurt sauce.

wild rice casserole

THIS RECIPE HAILS FROM MINNESOTA, ONE OF THE PRINCIPAL WILD RICE GROWING AREAS
OF THE U.S. **SERVES 4**

1 Tbsp (15 mL) butter

1 Tbsp (15 mL) olive oil

1 medium onion, finely chopped

1 medium red bell pepper, chopped

2 cups (500 mL) chopped mushrooms

1 cup (250 mL) pecan nuts, chopped
    roughly

1 cup (250 mL) wild rice

3 cups (750 mL) rich chicken or
    vegetable stock

¼ cup (60 mL) chopped fresh parsley

Salt and freshly ground black pepper

Chopped fresh parsley to garnish

1 Preheat the oven to 325°F (160°C). Heat the butter and oil together in a large flameproof casserole, add the onion and pepper, and cook slowly for about 5 minutes. Stir in the mushrooms and pecans and continue cooking until the juices run from the mushrooms, then add the wild rice. Stir well, then pour in the stock.

2 Bring to a boil and add the parsley. Cover and bake in the preheated oven for 1¼ to 1½ hours, until the rice has absorbed practically all the stock. Season to taste, and serve with a green salad.

chestnut and cranberry casserole

SLIGHTLY SWEET AND SOUR, THIS DISH IS FULL OF BRIGHT COLORS AND TEXTURES. **SERVES 6 TO 8**

1 large leek, trimmed and sliced

1 Tbsp (15 mL) oil

1 lb (450 g) peeled chestnuts, fresh
    or frozen

1 medium red bell pepper, seeded and
    chopped

1 medium zucchini, quartered and
    thickly sliced

4 sticks celery, chopped

⅓ cup (90 mL) raisins

1 Tbsp (15 mL) soy sauce

1 Tbsp (15 mL) chopped fresh cilantro

1 cinnamon stick, broken

2 cups (500 mL) rich vegetable stock

3 cups (750 mL) fresh or frozen
    cranberries

2 Tbsp (25 mL) raw sugar

Soy sauce to taste

Chopped fresh cilantro to garnish

1 Cook the leek in the oil until softened but not browned, then add the chestnuts and stir over the heat until defrosted, if frozen. Add the pepper, zucchini, and celery; stir-fry for 1 minute, then stir in all the remaining ingredients except the cranberries and sugar.

2 Bring the casserole to a boil, then simmer gently for 10 to 15 minutes. Add the cranberries; continue to cook for a further 10 minutes. Remove the cinnamon stick and add about 2 Tbsp (25 mL) of sugar. Stir in extra soy sauce to taste. Serve on a bed of boiled rice, topped with chopped cilantro.

peanut and bean sprout risotto

DRY-ROASTED JUMBO PEANUTS ADD A DELICIOUS CRUNCH TO THE DISH. **SERVES 4**

1½ cups (375 mL) brown rice

1 large onion, finely sliced

2 Tbsp (25 mL) olive oil

1 medium red bell pepper, seeded and sliced

1½ cups (375 mL) sliced mushrooms

3 Tbsp (45 mL) soy sauce

4 hard-boiled eggs

2 handfuls bean sprouts

1 cup (250 mL) unsalted dry-roasted jumbo peanuts

Salt and freshly ground black pepper

1 to 2 Tbsp (15 to 25mL) chopped cilantro

1 Bring the rice to a boil in a large pot of water, then simmer for 35 to 40 minutes, until tender. Drain well.

2 Cook the onion in the oil in a large skillet until softened but not browned. Add the pepper and cook for 1 to 2 minutes before adding the rice and mushrooms. Season with the soy sauce and stir-fry for 3 to 4 minutes, until the mushrooms are cooked and the rice has heated through.

3 Chop 3 of the hard-boiled eggs and add them to the pot with the bean sprouts and peanuts. Season the risotto with salt and pepper if necessary, then continue cooking for a further 1 to 2 minutes before adding the cilantro. Slice the remaining egg into quarters and use to garnish the risotto just before serving.

sweet and sour vegetable stir-fry

ALL THE STIR-FRIED VEGETABLES SHOULD BE CHOPPED TO THE SAME RELATIVE SIZE FOR EVEN COOKING. **SERVES 4**

1½ cups (375 mL) brown rice

1 cup (250 mL) carrot, julienned

1 small red onion, chopped

1 cup (250 mL) baby corn, halved

4 sticks celery, chopped

1 medium leek, trimmed and sliced

2 cups (500 mL) shredded bok choy

2 Tbsp (25 mL) sunflower or
   peanut oil

SAUCE

⅔ cup (150 mL) pineapple juice

1 Tbsp (15 mL) Demerara sugar

¼ cup (60 mL) white wine vinegar

¼ cup (60 mL) ketchup

Pinch of salt

Cilantro leaves and soy sauce

1 Bring the rice to a boil in a large pot of water and simmer for 30 minutes or until tender.

2 Meanwhile, prepare all the vegetables. Heat the oil in a large skillet or wok, then add the carrots, onion, corn, celery, and leek and stir-fry for 4 to 5 minutes, until starting to soften but still crisp. Blend the ingredients for the sauce together and add to the pot with the bok choy. Continue stir-frying for 2 to 3 minutes until the cabbage begins to wilt. Stir in the cilantro at the last moment.

3 Serve the stir-fry on a bed of the freshly cooked rice and spoon the sauce over. Provide soy sauce separately when you serve, for people to add if desired.

caramelized onion tart

THIS SAVORY FRENCH TART MAKES AN EXCELLENT LUNCH
DISH. **SERVES 6 TO 8**

5 cups (1.25 L) sliced onions

3 Tbsp (45 mL) olive oil

6 small cloves garlic, peeled and left whole

3 bay leaves

4 to 5 sprigs fresh thyme

Salt and freshly ground black pepper

BASE

⅓ cup (90 mL) toasted chopped hazelnuts or almonds

1 cup (250 mL) whole-wheat flour

½ tsp (2 mL) salt

1 egg, beaten

¼ cup (60 mL) olive oil

1 Cook the onions in the olive oil until they start to brown, then add the garlic, herbs, and seasonings. Cook slowly for at least 1 hour, until softened and lightly browned.

2 Meanwhile, make the base by blending the dry ingredients together, then binding them with the egg and olive oil. Work into a dough, then roll out to a rough circle about 10 in (25 cm) in diameter on a baking sheet. Chill for at least 45 minutes.

3 Preheat the oven to 425°F (220°C). Removing the bay leaves, spread the onion mixture over the nut base. Grind some black pepper over the onions, drizzle a little extra olive oil on top and bake for 25 minutes, until the base is lightly browned. Cool slightly before serving.

adzuki and fennel casserole

ADZUKI BEANS ARE VERY POPULAR IN CHINESE COOKING. I'VE COUPLED THEM HERE WITH THE EXOTIC FLAVORS OF THE PACIFIC RIM. **SERVES 6**

SALSA

1 medium orange

2 small tomatoes, chopped

½ small red onion or 4 scallions, finely chopped

1 small green chile, seeded and finely chopped

1 medium clove garlic, finely chopped

1 Tbsp (15 mL) chopped cilantro

1 medium green bell pepper, seeded and chopped

Salt and freshly ground black pepper

1 cup (250 mL) adzuki beans, soaked overnight and drained, or canned

1 medium onion, finely chopped

1 large bulb fennel, finely sliced

1 Tbsp (15 mL) oil

1 small red chile, seeded and finely chopped

1-in (2.5-cm) piece ginger root, peeled and finely sliced

2 medium cloves garlic, finely sliced

1 tsp (5 mL) Chinese 5-Spice powder

1 cinnamon stick, broken

½ tsp (2 mL) ground cloves

1 piece lemongrass, very finely chopped

1 cup (250 mL) orange juice

14-fl oz (398-mL) can chopped tomatoes

8-oz (250-g) can water chestnuts, drained and sliced

Soy sauce to taste

1 Prepare the salsa by grating the rind from the orange and chopping the flesh. Mix with the remaining ingredients and half the bell pepper. Set aside.

2 Drain the beans and rinse under cold water. Cook the onion and fennel in the oil until soft but not browned, then add the chile, ginger root, garlic, spices, and lemongrass. Cook slowly for 1 to 2 minutes, stirring, then add the beans, orange juice, and tomatoes. Bring to a boil, cover, and simmer gently for 30 minutes.

3 Stir in the remaining chopped pepper and the water chestnuts and continue cooking for a further 10 to 15 minutes, until the beans are tender. Season to taste with soy sauce and serve with the salsa.

chicken and lima bean bourguignon

A HEALTHY APPROACH TO THE CLASSIC RICH DISH FROM BURGUNDY, FRANCE. **SERVES 4**

⅔ cup (150 mL) lima beans, soaked
   overnight

1 Tbsp (15 mL) olive oil

1 Tbsp (15 mL) butter

4 large chicken thighs

1 large onion, finely chopped

2 strips bacon, diced

½ cup (125 mL) cognac

2 cloves garlic, crushed

4 sprigs fresh thyme

2 bay leaves

1 bouquet garni

Salt and freshly ground black pepper

1 Tbsp (15 mL) tomato paste

2 cups (500 mL) full-bodied red wine

1 cup (250 mL) sliced button
   mushrooms

Chicken stock as needed or water

Sour cream and chopped fresh chives
   to garnish

1 Preheat the oven to 350°F (175°C). Rinse the beans thoroughly then bring to a boil in a pot of fresh water. Simmer until required.

2 Heat the oil and butter together in a flameproof casserole, then add the chicken thighs and cook quickly until browned all over. Remove the chicken with a slotted spoon; add the onion and bacon and cook until softened but not browned. Return the chicken to the casserole and remove the pot from heat. Warm the cognac gently until it ignites. Pour the brandy into the pot and leave until the flames subside, then return the pot to the heat and add the garlic, herbs, and seasonings. Mix the tomato paste with the wine and pour into the pot, adding a little stock or water, if necessary, to cover the chicken. Bring to a boil, then cover the pot and cook in the preheated oven for 1½ hours.

3 Stir the mushrooms into the casserole; check the seasoning and that the beans are tender. Return the casserole to the oven for a further 15 to 20 minutes. Garnish with sour cream and chives.

chicken and kidney bean gumbo

A DELICIOUS HIGH-FIBER TAKE ON THE FAMOUS SOUTHERN
SPECIALITY. **SERVES 6**

1 large onion, finely sliced

3 sticks celery, sliced

2 Tbsp (25 mL) olive oil

1 lb (450 g) okra, trimmed and sliced

2 large cloves garlic, finely sliced

14-fl oz (398-mL) can chopped tomatoes

2 Tbsp (25 mL) butter

3 Tbsp (45 mL) whole-wheat flour

½ tsp (2 mL) chili powder

1 tsp (5 mL) ground cumin

4 sprigs fresh thyme

Salt and freshly ground black pepper

4 cups (1 L) rich chicken or vegetable stock

1 cup (250 mL) brown rice

1 cup (250 mL) cooked chicken

14-oz (400-g) can kidney beans, drained

1 cup (250 mL) shrimp

Hot pepper sauce

1 Cook the onion and celery in the oil for about 5 minutes until starting to soften but not browned. Add the okra and garlic and cook for a further 3 minutes before adding the tomatoes. Cover the pot and simmer slowly for 15 minutes.

2 Prepare the sauce while the okra mixture is cooking. Melt the butter in a large flameproof casserole dish, then stir in the flour, spices, herbs, and seasonings off the heat. Cook slowly for 2 to 3 minutes then gradually add the stock, again off the heat. Bring to a boil, stirring, then simmer for 2 minutes before adding the okra mixture. Season, return to a boil, then cover and simmer for 1 hour.

3 After 30 minutes, bring the rice to a boil in a pot of water, then simmer for 30 to 40 minutes, until tender. Add the chopped chicken and kidney beans to the gumbo. Return to a boil and simmer for 10 minutes, then add the shrimp and cook for a further 5 minutes. Season to taste, adding pepper sauce as required, and serve garnished with spoonfuls of the cooked rice.

chicken and vegetable fricassee

THE CHICKEN MAY BE REPLACED BY COOKED BEANS IF PREFERRED. **SERVES 4**

1 Tbsp (15 mL) oil

1 cup (250 mL) cooked chicken, shredded

1¼ lb (600 g) prepared mixed vegetables, diced or sliced

½ cup (125 mL) dry white wine

1 cup (250 mL) sour cream

Salt and freshly ground black pepper

Chopped fresh parsley

1 Heat the oil in a skillet; add the chicken and cook quickly until starting to brown, then add the prepared vegetables, tossing them in the hot juices. Cover the skillet and cook slowly for about 8 to 10 minutes, until the vegetables have softened in the steam.

2 Pour the wine into the skillet and cook quickly, stirring all the time, until the wine has reduced by half. Stir in the sour cream, season to taste, then heat gently without boiling. Serve with rice, garnished with chopped parsley.

cassoulet

THIS CLASSIC FRENCH DISH IS WELL WORTH THE LENGTHY BUT NOT DIFFICULT PREPARATION. **SERVES 8**

2 cups (500 mL) navy beans, soaked overnight

2 large onions, finely sliced

3 Tbsp (45 mL) olive oil

2 cloves garlic, crushed

5 cups (1.25 L) diced cooked meats (e.g., chicken, ham, garlic sausage, goose, duck)

Salt and freshly ground black pepper

½ cup (1.25 mL) chopped fresh parsley

3 medium tomatoes, chopped

4 cups (1 L) rich chicken or vegetable stock

2 cups (500 mL) whole-wheat bread crumbs

1 Drain the beans and rinse them thoroughly under cold running water. Bring to a boil in a pot of fresh water, then cover and simmer for 1½ hours, until tender. Drain and keep until required.

2 Preheat the oven to 325°F (160°C). Cook the onions in the oil in a large flameproof casserole dish until lightly browned, then add the garlic. Remove from the heat and add the meats in a thick layer, seasoning with a little salt and pepper and about half the parsley. Layer the tomatoes on top of the meats, then cover with the cooked beans. Sprinkle with the remaining parsley and with plenty of seasoning, then add the stock, which should come to just below the level of the beans. Bring to a boil, cover, and bake for 1½ hours.

3 Remove the lid. Make a thick layer of bread crumbs over the cassoulet and return it to the oven for a further 20 to 30 minutes, uncovered, until the bread crumbs have browned lightly. Serve immediately while still hot.

chicken and sweet potato curry

BLEND THE SAUCE INGREDIENTS TO A THICK PASTE BEFORE COOKING. **SERVES 4**

SAUCE

1 large onion

3 cloves garlic

1 green chile, seeded and roughly chopped

2 Tbsps tomato paste

1 Tbsp mild curry powder

1 Tbsp lime pickle or spiced fruit chutney

1 tsp Demerara sugar

1 tsp salt

1-inch piece fresh ginger root, peeled and chopped

2 chicken breast fillets, skinned and diced

3 Tbsps sunflower oil

2 cups diced sweet potato

2 cups water

Salt

⅓ cup fresh cilantro leaves, torn

1 Purée all the ingredients for the sauce together in a blender or food processor until a thick paste forms. Cook the chicken in the oil in a large skillet until it starts to brown, then add the sweet potato and cook until lightly browned.

2 Spoon the curry paste into the skillet and cook slowly for 2 to 3 minutes. Stir in the water. Simmer slowly for 20 to 25 minutes, until the chicken is tender. Add a little more water, if necessary, during cooking. Season to taste with salt, then add the cilantro and serve.

chicken and flageolet bean risotto

ALWAYS USE ARBORIO RICE FOR RISOTTO TO GET THE MOIST, CREAMY TEXTURE THE DISH IS FAMED FOR. **SERVES 4**

½ cup (125 mL) flageolet or white kidney beans,
    soaked overnight or canned

2 medium chicken breasts or 4 medium chicken thighs,
    skinned, boned, and diced

1 Tbsp (15 mL) olive oil

1 large onion, chopped

1 medium red bell pepper, seeded and chopped

2 plump cloves garlic, finely sliced

2 cups (500 mL) arborio rice,
    white or brown

5 cups (1.25 mL) rich chicken or vegetable stock

1 cup (250 mL) dry white wine

1 cup (250 mL) frozen or fresh peas

Salt and freshly ground black pepper

2 Tbsp (25 mL) chopped fresh Italian parsley

1 Drain the beans and rinse them thoroughly under cold running water. Place in a pot of fresh water, bring to a boil and cover to simmer for 1 to 1¼ hours, until tender.

2 Brown the chicken in the oil in a large skillet, then add the onion and cook until soft but not browned. Stir in the pepper and garlic and cook for a further 2 minutes. Add the rice, toss it in the juices and cook for 1 minute. Add 2 cups (500 mL) of stock and bring to a boil, stirring all the time, then simmer until the stock is absorbed, stirring occasionally. Add 2 more cups (500 mL) of stock and cook until absorbed, then add the wine and repeat the process for a second time.

3 Stir the peas into the risotto with the remaining stock and cook, stirring constantly, until the stock is almost absorbed and the risotto is thick and creamy. Season to taste, and stir in the parsley just before serving.

ABOVE SHRIMP CHOW MEIN

spiced chicken with cabbage

A SATISFYING DISH THAT IS BEST SERVED WITH BOILED RICE. **SERVES 4**

1 medium onion, finely sliced

1 Tbsp (15 mL) peanut oil

1½ cups (375 mL) shredded cooked chicken

½ tsp (2 mL) curry powder

1 small green chile, seeded and finely chopped

2 cloves garlic, finely sliced

2 cups (500 mL) green beans, cut into 1-in (2.5-cm) lengths

2 cups (500 mL) shredded cabbage

1 to 2 Tbsp (15 to 25 mL) peanut butter, according to taste

14-fl oz (398-mL) can chopped tomatoes

Salt and freshly ground black pepper

1 Cook the onion in the oil until it starts to brown, then add the chicken. Cook quickly for 2 or 3 minutes to heat the chicken through. Stir in the curry powder and cook slowly for 1 minute. Add the chile, garlic, and green beans and stir-fry for 1 to 2 minutes.

2 Next, add the shredded cabbage, peanut butter, and tomatoes, then simmer for 6 to 8 minutes, until the cabbage just starts to soften. Season to taste with salt and freshly ground black pepper, then serve on a bed of boiled brown rice.

shrimp chow mein

IF USING FROZEN SHRIMP, DEFROST THEM BEFORE USING FOR BEST RESULTS. **SERVES 4**

3 sheets thread egg noodles

1 large onion, chopped

2 Tbsp (25 mL) sunflower or peanut oil

1 tsp (5 mL) Chinese 5-Spice powder

1 cup (250 mL) zucchini, julienned

1 cup (250 mL) carrot, julienned

1 small green bell pepper, seeded and julienned

1 small red chile, seeded and finely chopped (optional)

2 plump cloves garlic, finely sliced

2 cups (500 mL) peeled shrimp

2 large handfuls bean sprouts

¼ cup (60 mL) sherry

¼ cup (60 mL) soy sauce

½ cup (125 mL) water

1 Soak the noodles in boiling water until needed, stirring them occasionally to separate the strands. Cook the onion in the oil in a large skillet until softened but not browned. Stir in the 5-Spice powder and cook for a further 1 minute.

2 Add the zucchini, carrot, pepper, chile, and garlic, and stir-fry for 3 to 4 minutes. Drain the noodles and add them to the skillet with the shrimp and bean sprouts. Mix the sherry, soy sauce, and water together and pour the mixture into the pot. Cook for 2 to 3 minutes, tossing the vegetables and noodles together in the sauce. Serve piping hot, with extra soy sauce, if you like.

trout with wild rice stuffing

THE CRUMBLY RICE STUFFING GOES WELL WITH THE
DELICATE FISH. **SERVES 4**

STUFFING

1 small onion, finely chopped

1 stick celery, finely sliced

1 Tbsp (15 mL) oil

½ small green bell pepper, finely chopped

1 small clove garlic, crushed

1½ cups (375 mL) cooked wild rice (about ⅓ cup/ 150 mL raw)

1 Tbsp (15 mL) chopped fresh dill or parsley

Grated rind and juice of 1 lemon

Salt and freshly ground black pepper

4 trout, brown or rainbow

1 Preheat the oven to 400°F (200°C). Lightly butter a suitable ovenproof dish.

2 Cook the onion and celery in the oil until softened but not browned. Add the pepper and continue cooking until all the vegetables are tender. Remove the pot from the heat and stir in the garlic and cooked rice. Add the herbs, lemon rind and juice, then season to taste with salt and freshly ground black pepper.

3 Clean the trout, removing the heads if preferred. Season the cavities lightly and fill with the stuffing. Arrange the fish in the prepared dish and cover with foil. Bake for 15 to 20 minutes, according to the size of the fish, until just cooked. Serve immediately while still hot.

stir-fried trout

THE ONLY WAY TO BETTER THIS IS TO USE FRESHLY-CAUGHT TROUT. **SERVES 2 TO 3**

3 Tbsp (45 mL) oil

4 cups (1 L) mixed stir-fry vegetables

1 medium onion, cut into wedges

1 chile, seeded and chopped

2 large trout fillets, about 1 lb
  (450 g), skinned and cut into 2-in
  (5-cm) pieces

7-oz (200-g) can water chestnuts,
  drained and halved

2 handfuls bean sprouts

2 Tbsp (25 mL) soy sauce

1 Tbsp (15 mL) chile sauce

1 Heat the oil in a wok or a large skillet until almost smoking. Add the prepared vegetables, onion, and chile, and stir-fry for 1 minute.

2 Add the trout and water chestnuts, and continue cooking over very high heat for 2 to 3 minutes, until the fish is almost cooked – don't stir too vigorously or the fish will break up. Finally, add the bean sprouts, soy and chile sauces and cook for a further 1 minute. Serve immediately over brown rice or noodles.

spanish-style haddock

SERVE WITH CRUSTY WHOLE-WHEAT BREAD FOR A SUMMER LUNCH OR LIGHT SUPPER. **SERVES 4**

1 lb (450 g) thick haddock fillet or
  similar white fish, skinned

3 Tbsp (45 mL) fruity olive oil

1 small mild onion, finely sliced

2 plump cloves garlic, finely sliced

1 cup (250 mL) sliced mushrooms

1 small red bell pepper, seeded and
  sliced

1 small green bell pepper, seeded and
  sliced

Salt and freshly ground black pepper

½ cup (125 mL) white wine vinegar

⅓ cup (90 mL) water

1 Tbsp (15 mL) sugar

1 Cut the fish into bite-sized pieces. Heat two tablespoons of the oil in a skillet and fry the fish until just cooked. Transfer it to a glass dish. Heat the remaining oil in the skillet; add the onion and garlic and cook until soft but not browned. Stir in the mushrooms and peppers and cook for a further 1 to 2 minutes – the vegetables should retain a crisp texture. Spoon the vegetables over the fish and season lightly.

2 Pour the vinegar and water into the skillet and bring to a boil. Stir in the sugar until dissolved, then pour the liquid over the fish and vegetables. Leave to cool, then cover and place in the refrigerator for 24 hours.

lamb with lentils and prunes

RELISH THE CLASSIC FLAVORS OF SOUTHWEST FRANCE IN THIS TASTY CASSEROLE. **SERVES 4**

1 Tbsp (15 mL) olive oil

1 Tbsp (15 mL) butter

4 lamb chops or 1 lb (450 g) lamb fillet, cut into 4 pieces

1 large onion, sliced

3 sticks celery, sliced

2 large carrots, sliced

2 plump cloves garlic, finely sliced

1 Tbsp (15 mL) whole-wheat flour

2 cups (500 mL) rich vegetable or lamb stock

1 cup (500 mL) dried prunes

½ cup (125 mL) green lentils

6 juniper berries, lightly crushed

4 to 5 sprigs fresh thyme

Salt and freshly ground black pepper

1 Preheat the oven to 325°F (160°C). Heat the oil and butter in a flameproof casserole dish and brown the lamb on all sides. Remove the meat with a slotted spoon and set aside until needed. Add the onion to the casserole and cook slowly until softened but not browned, then add the celery, carrot, and garlic and continue cooking for a further 2 to 3 minutes.

2 Stir the flour into the vegetables and cook for 1 to 2 minutes, then gradually add the stock, stirring to scrape the bottom of the pot. Bring to a boil; add the prunes and lentils and simmer for 2 to 3 minutes. Return the lamb to the casserole and add the remaining seasonings. Cover and cook in the preheated oven for 1½ to 2 hours. Season to taste before serving.

apple ratatouille with spiced pork

CIDER, APPLE, AND CORN COMPLEMENT THE PORK
WELL. **SERVES 4**

MARINADE

¼ **cup (60 mL) black bean or hoisin sauce**

2 tsp (10 mL) Thai 7-Spice seasoning

2 Tbsp (25 mL) soy sauce

12 oz (375 g) pork fillet or tenderloin, in one thick piece if possible

½ **cup (125 mL) black beans soaked overnight, or canned**

1 large onion, finely sliced

3 Tbsp (45 mL) oil

2 to 3 plump cloves garlic, finely sliced

1 small eggplant, sliced

1 small green bell pepper, seeded and sliced

1 cup (250 mL) baby corn cobs, halved

14-fl oz (398-mL) can chopped tomatoes

1 large Granny Smith apple, peeled, cored and sliced

1 cup (250 mL) dry cider or apple juice

1 Mix together the ingredients for the marinade, then add the pork and coat thoroughly with the mixture. Leave to stand for at least 1 hour, turning the pork once or twice.

2 Drain the beans and rinse them thoroughly under cold running water. Bring to a boil in a pot of fresh water then cover and simmer gently until required.

3 Preheat the oven to 400°F (200°C). Transfer the pork to a small roasting pot and spoon the marinade over. Roast in the preheated oven for 30 minutes. Cook the onion in the oil in a large pot until softened but not browned, then add the remaining ratatouille vegetables, the apple, and the cider. Drain the beans, add them to the pot, then bring to a boil. Simmer for about 20 minutes, until the beans and the vegetables are tender. Slice the pork thinly and serve it with the ratatouille and baked or mashed potatoes.

spiced lamb with chickpeas

A SPICY STEW, RICH WITH MIDDLE EASTERN FLAVORS. **SERVES 6**

½ cup (125 mL) chickpeas, soaked overnight or canned

8 oz (250 g) lamb, sliced

3 Tbsp (45 mL) olive oil

1 medium onion, finely sliced

1 small eggplant, finely sliced

2 tsp (10 mL) ground cumin

1 tsp (5 mL) allspice

1 cinnamon stick, broken

⅔ cup (150 mL) red wine

14-fl oz (398-mL) can chopped tomatoes

1 cup (250 mL) rich vegetable or lamb stock

½ cup (125 mL) dried apricots

Salt and freshly ground black pepper

2 cups (500 mL) couscous

⅓ cup (90 mL) pistachios, unsalted

Olive oil

Chopped fresh parsley

1 Drain the chickpeas and rinse thoroughly. Bring to a boil in a pot of fresh water, cover and simmer for 30 to 40 minutes.

2 Fry the lamb in the oil in a pot until browned on all sides, then remove from the pot with a slotted spoon and set aside. Add the onion and eggplant to the oil and cook over high heat until golden brown, adding a little extra oil if necessary. Stir in the spices and continue cooking over very low heat for 1 to 2 minutes.

3 Return the lamb to the pot and add the wine. Bring to a boil and simmer until well reduced, scraping the bottom of the pot. Stir in the tomatoes, stock, and apricots and seasoning. Add the drained beans, cover and simmer for 30 minutes.

4 After 20 minutes, pour a little warm water over the couscous and leave for 10 minutes. Transfer to a steamer tier. Stir the nuts into the stew; place the couscous over the pot, cover and cook 15 to 20 minutes. Dress the couscous with olive oil and season. Season the stew and serve on a bed of couscous. Garnish with parsley.

thai-style beef

USE RICE OR NOODLES INSTEAD OF POTATOES IF YOU
PREFER. **SERVES 4**

1 lb (450 g) small new potatoes in their skins

3 Tbsp (45 mL) corn oil

8 thin slices sirloin or flank steak, cut into strips

3 cups (375 mL) broccoli florets and stalks, roughly chopped

⅔ cup (150 mL) scallions, chopped

2 cups (500 mL) sliced mushrooms

1 piece lemongrass, trimmed and sliced

2 medium cloves garlic, finely sliced

1 cup (250 mL) salted cashew nuts

½ cup (125 mL) oyster sauce

¼ cup (60 mL) water

½ cup (125 mL) chopped cilantro

1 Bring the potatoes to a boil in a pot of water, then simmer for 10 minutes. Drain and leave until cool enough to handle, then slice in half lengthways.

2 Heat the oil in a large wok or skillet, then add the beef and stir-fry for 1 minute. Add the prepared vegetables with the lemongrass and garlic, and continue cooking for a further 3 to 4 minutes. Stir the potatoes into the pot with the cashews, oyster sauce, and water, then cook for a further 1 to 2 minutes until the sauce is bubbling. Add the cilantro immediately before serving.

4 Desserts

When time allows, dessert is the perfect ending to a good meal, a treat to be thoroughly enjoyed. Many of the desserts included here contain fruit. Berries and exotic fruits, such as mangoes, are best eaten in a simple fruit salad, especially if they are fully ripened, but using just a few fruits rather than filling a bowl with numerous varieties can produce a stylish, light dessert; for example, strawberries served with melon and orange. Make a change by serving a flavored, blended cream instead of whipped cream – lime mascarpone is perfect with a dish of peaches and raspberries, for example.

Raspberries and blackberries are expensive to buy, even when they are in season, as they are time consuming to pick and have a very short shelf life. I usually buy them frozen in fruit mixes; then they are reasonably priced and make a wonderful base for any number of desserts.

Beans are not usually the first choice of ingredients for a dessert, but adzuki beans, which are semi-sweet, are good in both savory and sweet dishes. The Apple Bean Betty that I have included here is delicious and I thoroughly recommend it. Although white rice does not contain as much fiber as brown, it is still a source of fiber and should not be disregarded in a high-fiber diet. I am a rice pudding addict and have included an everyday rice pudding, as well as a much creamier pudding with fresh mangoes and grapes stirred into it.

LEFT SUMMER FRUIT UPSIDE-DOWN TRIFLE (SEE PAGE 170)

plum and apple pudding

IN COLD WEATHER YOU CAN'T BEAT A WARM
SPONGE PUDDING. **SERVES 4 TO 6**

2 lb (900 g) ripe plums and Granny Smith apples, mixed

¼ cup (60 mL) light brown sugar

TOPPING

½ cup (125 mL) margarine

½ cup (125 mL) light brown sugar

1 large egg, beaten

1¼ cups (300 mL) whole-wheat flour

1 tsp (5 mL) baking powder

Pinch of salt

1 tsp (5 mL) ground ginger

1 Tbsp (15 mL) milk

1 Preheat the oven to 375°F (190°C). Peel, core, and slice the apples, then cut the plums in half and remove the stones. Cut the plums into quarters if they are very firm. Mix the fruits and place in a suitable ovenproof dish – I use an 8-in (20-cm), round flan dish – then sprinkle the sugar on top.

2 Cream the margarine and sugar for the topping until pale and creamy, then beat in the egg. Mix the flour, baking powder, salt, and ginger, then fold into the egg mixture with the milk. Spoon the mixture as evenly as possible over the fruit. Bake in the preheated oven for about 30 to 35 minutes, until the pudding is set and shrinking slightly from the sides of the dish. Serve hot.

banana bran custard

QUICK TO MAKE, THIS DESSERT WILL KEEP REFRIGERATED FOR UP TO 2 DAYS. **SERVES 4**

2 medium bananas, sliced

Grated rind and juice of 1 lemon

⅔ cup (150 mL) sour cream or yogurt

⅓ cup (90 mL) pecans, chopped

1 Tbsp (15 mL) honey

¼ cup (60 mL) wheat or oat bran

Milk

1 In a bowl, toss the banana slices in lemon juice, then carefully mix in the cream or yogurt, nuts, honey, and bran. If the mixture is very thick, add 1 to 2 tablespoons of milk to thin it down.

2 Decorate with the lemon rind just before serving. If serving immediately, the honey may be drizzled over the cream in a zigzag pattern.

rum and raisin yogurt ice cream

THIS MAKES A FULL-BODIED, BUT NOT TOO RICH, DELICIOUS DESSERT. **SERVES 6 TO 8**

½ cup (125 mL) seedless raisins

¼ cup (60 mL) rum

2 large egg whites

½ cup (125 mL) light brown sugar

⅓ cup (90 mL) water

⅔ cup (150 mL) thick plain yogurt

1¼ cups (300 mL) whipping cream

1 Soak the raisins in the rum for 20 minutes before beginning the ice cream.

2 Whisk the egg whites until stiff. At the same time, heat the sugar with the water until the sugar has dissolved, then bring the syrup to a boil and boil rapidly for 3 minutes. Beating continuously, pour the sugar syrup in a steady stream onto the whisked egg whites; continue beating for about 1 minute. Add the yogurt and continue beating until the mixture is cool; this is best done in a mixer.

3 Whisk the whipping cream until thick and floppy but not stiff. Drain the rum from the raisins and into the yogurt mixture; add the cream, and, finally, fold in the raisins. Turn the mixture into a bombe mold or a suitable container and freeze for about 4 hours, until firm. Remove from the freezer 20 minutes before required, to allow it to soften.

vanilla ice cream

THIS POPULAR VICTORIAN DESSERT HAS RECENTLY ENJOYED A GREAT REVIVAL. **SERVES 6 TO 8**

2 cups (500 mL) milk

1 vanilla bean

4 egg yolks

½ cup (125 mL) light brown sugar

⅔ cup (150 mL) whipping cream

1 cup (250 mL) whole-wheat bread crumbs, evenly toasted

1 Heat the milk with the vanilla bean until almost at a boil, then leave to stand for 10 minutes before removing the vanilla. Beat the egg yolks with the sugar until a thick paste. Return the milk to the heat and bring almost to simmering point, then pour onto the egg yolks in a steady stream, beating all the time. Rinse the pot, return the custard to it, and heat gently, stirring until the mixture coats the back of a wooden spoon. Do not be tempted to overcook the custard or it will curdle. Pour the custard into a bowl and allow to cool completely.

2 Chill the custard in a freezer for 1½ hours, until thick and slushy. Whip the cream until soft and floppy. Fold it into the custard with the bread crumbs, then return the ice cream to the freezer. Stir after 1 hour, then leave for a further 2 to 3 hours until completely set.

3 Remove the ice cream from the freezer about 30 minutes before serving, to allow it to soften.

apricot bread and butter pudding

TUCK THE FRUIT INTO THE PUDDING SO THAT IT WON'T BURN
DURING COOKING. **SERVES 4**

3 to 4 slices whole-wheat bread

Margarine or butter

½ cup (125 mL) roughly chopped dried apricots

¼ cup (60 mL) golden raisins

2 cups (500 mL) milk

3 large eggs

1 Tbsp (15 mL) light brown sugar

1 Tbsp (15 mL) yogurt

Demerara sugar, to top

Cinnamon, to top

1 Preheat the oven to 350°F (175°C). Butter the bread and cut it into triangular quarters. Arrange half the bread in the bottom of a large pie dish. Scatter the dried fruits over, then top with the remaining bread. Beat the milk with the eggs and sugar then pour over the pudding – if you leave the crusts on the bread, I suggest leaving the pudding to stand for 15 to 20 minutes before cooking, to allow the crusts to soften.

2 Bake the pudding for 35 to 40 minutes, until the custard is set. Serve warm, not hot, with a dollop of yogurt and dusted with demerara sugar and cinnamon.

apricot cheesecake

ALWAYS USE GELATIN WITHIN SIX MONTHS OF PURCHASE. **SERVES 8 TO 10**

BASE

¼ cup (60 mL) butter

¼ cup (60 mL) honey

2 cups (500 mL) granola

1½ cups (375 mL) dried apricots,
    soaked for 4 hours

1½ cups (375 mL) water

1 cup (250 mL) low-fat cream
    cheese, or strained cottage cheese

1 cup (250 mL) thick plain yogurt

1 Tbsp (15 mL) powdered gelatin

2 large egg whites

Fine strips of orange rind

1 Melt the butter in a pan, then mix well with the honey and granola. Press and smooth the mixture into the base of a deep, 8-in (20-cm), springform or loose-bottomed cake pan. Chill until required.

2 Reserve ⅓ cup (90 mL) of liquid from the apricots. Purée the fruit with the remaining juice in a blender or food processor until smooth – add a little extra water if necessary to achieve a smooth paste. Turn into a bowl and beat in the cheese and yogurt.

3 Heat the reserved apricot juice until almost at a boil in a small pot, then remove from the heat and sprinkle the gelatin over. Stir until almost dissolved then leave to stand for 2 minutes, until completely dissolved. Stir one heaping tablespoon (15 mL) of the apricot mixture into the gelatin – this helps to incorporate it evenly – then fold the gelatin into the apricot mixture. Whisk the egg whites until stiff, and fold them into the apricots.

4 Pour the mixture over the granola base and smooth the top. Chill in the refrigerator for 2 to 3 hours until set. Carefully remove the cheesecake from the pot and decorate with strips of orange rind just before serving.

prune and walnut tart

BAKED IN CRISP PASTRY, THIS CREAMY TART IS GREAT FOR A SPECIAL OCCASION. **SERVES 6**

PASTRY

½ cup (125 mL) butter

1¼ cups (300 mL) whole-wheat flour

1 Tbsp (15 mL) light brown sugar

1 large egg, beaten

FILLING

2 Tbsp (25 mL) plum jam or apple jelly

⅔ cup (150 mL) pitted prunes, chopped

⅓ cup (90 mL) walnut pieces, chopped

1¼ cups (300 mL) milk or light cream

2 large eggs, beaten

1 tsp (5 mL) superfine sugar (optional)

Freshly grated nutmeg

1 Prepare the pastry by blending the butter into the flour and sugar. Bind with the beaten egg, then knead gently on a lightly floured surface. Cover the pastry with plastic wrap and chill in a refrigerator for 30 minutes.

2 Preheat the oven to 400°F (200°C). Roll out the pastry to line a deep 8-in (20-cm) flan or cake pan, preferably with a loose base. Line the pastry tin with baking parchment and dry beans, then bake for 15 minutes. Remove the beans and parchment, and continue cooking for a further 5 minutes, until the base is dry.

3 Reduce the oven heat to 350°F (175°C). Spread the jam over the base of the flan and top with the prunes and walnuts. Beat the milk or cream with the eggs and sugar, if used, and pour the custard into the flan and sprinkle with nutmeg. Bake for 40 minutes, or until lightly set. Serve warm or cold.

strawberry and orange trifle

THE PAIRING OF STRAWBERRY AND ORANGE IS OUTSTANDING. **SERVES 4**

3 cups (750 mL) strawberries, topped

Grated rind and juice of 2 medium oranges

½ cup (125 mL) Demerara sugar

1 cup (250 mL) Devon cream

1 cup (250 mL) thick plain yogurt

1 Tbsp (15 mL) Demerara sugar

1 Tbsp (15 mL) wheat or oat bran

1 Simmer the strawberries with the orange rind, juice, and sugar until just soft. Allow the fruit to cool, then fold it into the cream. Blend in the yogurt, either mixing it completely or leaving it marbled through the cream mixture. Spoon into a glass serving bowl or individual dishes and chill for 1 hour.

2 Mix the remaining tablespoon of sugar with the bran and scatter over the trifle before serving.

baked bananas with rum

THE NATURAL SWEETNESS OF RAISINS AND COCONUT MEANS NO ADDED SUGAR! **SERVES 4**

4 large ripe bananas

½ cup (125 mL) orange juice

2 Tbsp (25 mL) rum

¼ cup (60 mL) seedless raisins

¼ cup (60 mL) dried coconut

Vanilla ice cream

1 Preheat the oven to 375°F (190°C). Peel the bananas, cut them in half lengthways, then place in a suitable ovenproof dish that is just large enough for them. Mix the orange juice and rum and pour over the bananas. Sprinkle with the raisins and coconut.

2 Bake in the preheated oven for 15 minutes, or until the bananas are soft. Serve immediately with the ice cream.

mango yogurt brulée

A DELICIOUS VARIATION ON CRÊME BRULÉE. **SERVES 4**

1 large ripe mango

1½ cups (375 mL) thick plain yogurt

3 Tbsp (45 mL) All-Bran® cereal, crushed

½ cup (125 mL) Demerara sugar

1 Peel the mango, remove the stone, and chop the flesh, then divide it among 4 ovenproof ramekin dishes.

2 Preheat the broiler. Blend the yogurt with the cereal, breaking the strands into smaller pieces, then spoon it over the fruit. Spoon a thick layer of sugar over the yogurt, so that it is covered.

3 Cook the puddings under the hot broiler for 1 to 2 minutes, until the sugar has melted. Do not overcook, or the yogurt will bubble up through the sugar. Allow to cool, then chill for at least 1 hour before serving.

date and ginger pudding

ON A TOTALLY DECADENT DAY, SERVE WITH TOFFEE OR BUTTERSCOTCH SAUCE. **SERVES 6 TO 8**

⅓ cup (90 mL) pitted dates, chopped

2 pieces preserved stem ginger, finely chopped

1 ripe banana, mashed

2 Tbsp (25 mL) ginger syrup (from the bottle of stem ginger)

½ cup (125 mL) margarine or butter

½ cup (125 mL) light brown sugar

2 large eggs, beaten

1½ cups (375 mL) whole-wheat flour

1½ tsp (7 mL) baking powder

Pinch of salt

2 Tbsp (25 mL) milk

1 Preheat the oven to 375°F (190°C), then lightly grease and line a deep 7-in (18-cm) cake pan.

2 Mix together the dates, ginger, banana, and ginger syrup. Cream the margarine and sugar together until pale and creamy, then beat in the eggs a little at a time. Mix together the flour, baking powder, and salt and fold into the egg mixture. Fold in the date and banana mix, then add a little milk to give a soft, dropping consistency.

3 Turn into the prepared pan and smooth the top. Bake in the preheated oven for 30 to 35 minutes, until a toothpick inserted into the center comes out clean, and the pudding shrinks away from the sides of the tin. Serve cut into wedges with cream.

warm spiced compote

THE MORE TYPES OF FRUIT, THE TASTIER THE DISH. **SERVES 6**

2 cups (500 mL) chopped dried mixed fruits

1 cup (250 mL) water

1½ cups (375 mL) orange juice

½ tsp (2 mL) cardamom seeds

1 cinnamon stick, broken

Thick plain yogurt

⅓ cup (90 mL) chopped brazil nuts

1 Place the fruits in a small pot with the water and orange juice. Crush the cardamom seeds lightly and add them to the fruit with the cinnamon stick. Heat gently until almost at a boil, then remove the pot from the heat, cover, and leave to stand for 3 to 4 hours.

2 Remove the cinnamon stick and reheat the fruit gently before serving, topped with yogurt and chopped brazil nuts.

carrot pudding

A GREAT DESSERT TO FOLLOW A CURRY OR SPICY DISH. **SERVES 3 TO 4**

1½ cups (375 mL) milk

½ tsp (2 mL) cardamom seeds

1 cinnamon stick, broken

6 cloves

1 cup (250 mL) grated carrot

¼ cup (60 mL) shelled unsalted
   pistachios

⅓ cup (90 mL) pitted dates, chopped

1 tsp (5 mL) light brown sugar

3 large eggs, beaten

1 Heat the milk with the spices until almost at a boil, then remove from the heat and leave to stand 20 minutes before straining. Preheat the oven to 325°F (160°C).

2 Mix the carrot, pistachios, and dates and transfer to a lightly greased pie dish. Beat the sugar with the eggs, then add the strained milk. Pour the mixture over the carrots, stir briefly, and bake in the preheated oven for about 1½ hours, or until set. Serve warm with a sweet cookie, such as shortbread.

sweet fruit pilaf

A CREAMY RICE PUDDING ENHANCED BY TROPICAL FRUITS. **SERVES 4**

⅓ cup (90 mL) short-grain rice

1 Tbsp (15 mL) light brown sugar

6 cloves

2 bay leaves

2 cups (500 mL) milk

1 cup (250 mL) light cream

1 small orange

1 large ripe mango, chopped

⅔ cup (150 mL) seedless grapes,
   halved

1 Preheat the oven to 300°F (150°C). Place the rice in a large ovenproof dish with the sugar and spices, then add the milk and cream. Stir briefly and bake in the preheated oven for 2 hours. The rice will be creamier and wetter than for a traditional rice pudding.

2 Remove the skin and bay leaves from the pudding; leave for 20 minutes to cool. Meanwhile, prepare the fruit. Grate the rind from the orange and reserve it for decoration, then peel the fruit and chop the flesh roughly. Mix the orange with the mango and grapes, then stir the fruit into the warm rice. Serve immediately.

apple bean betty

ADZUKI BEANS ARE SLIGHTLY SWEET AND MAKE A DELICIOUS DESSERT BASE FOR THIS VERSION OF THE AMERICAN CLASSIC. **SERVES 6**

⅓ cup (90 mL) adzuki beans, soaked overnight, or canned

½ tsp (2 mL) ground cinnamon

¼ cup (60 mL) honey

2 cups (500 mL) finely sliced baking apples

CRUMBLE

⅓ cup (90 mL) butter

1 cup (250 mL) whole-wheat flour

½ cup (125 mL) All-Bran® cereal

1 Tbsp (15 mL) light brown sugar

1 Drain the adzuki beans, then rinse them under cold running water. Bring to a boil in a pot of fresh water, cover and simmer for 30 minutes or until tender. Drain and set to one side.

2 Preheat the oven to 375°F (190°C). Combine the cinnamon and honey and mix into the apples and adzuki beans in a suitable ovenproof dish. Blend the butter into the flour, All-Bran®, and sugar, then spoon the crumble mixture over the fruit. Bake in the preheated oven for 30 to 35 minutes, until the crumble has browned and set. Serve with custard, cream, or yogurt.

fresh apricots with dried cherries and ginger

CHERRIES AND GINGER DRAW OUT THE FLAVOR OF THE APRICOTS. **SERVES 4**

- **8 large ripe apricots**
- **⅓ cup (90 mL) dried cherries, chopped**
- **4 pieces preserved stem ginger, finely chopped**
- **4 Tbsp (50 mL) ginger syrup (from the bottle of stem ginger)**

1 Cut the apricots in half and remove the pits – cut the fruit into quarters if they are very large. Add the cherries, the ginger, and the syrup from the ginger to the apricots.

2 Stir the fruit gently to coat it all in ginger syrup. Chill for no more than 45 minutes before serving.

banana and rhubarb trifle

TOSS THE BANANA SLICES IN LIME JUICE TO PREVENT THEM FROM BROWNING. **SERVES 6**

- **2 cups (500 mL) cooked rhubarb pieces, fresh or canned**
- **2 cups (500 mL) sliced ripe banana**
- **½ cup (125 mL) rhubarb juice or syrup, from the cooking process or the can**
- **Grated rind and juice of 1 lime**
- **2 pieces preserved stem ginger, finely chopped**
- **¼ cup (60 mL) honey**
- **1 cup (250 mL) thick plain yogurt**
- **¼ cup (60 mL) wheat germ**

1 Purée the rhubarb, banana, rhubarb juice, lime rind, and juice in a blender or food processor. Turn into a bowl and add the ginger with honey to taste.

2 Fold the yogurt into the mixture with the wheat germ, then cover and chill for 1 to 2 hours. Serve decorated with a little extra wheat germ or lime zest.

strawberries with melon and orange

MELONS ARE MOSTLY WATER, BUT MIXED WITH BERRIES THEY MAKE A GREAT FIBER-RICH DESSERT. **SERVES 4**

3 cups (750 mL) halved fresh strawberries

1 small honeydew or cantaloupe melon, balled

2 small oranges

¼ cup (60 mL) orange juice (optional)

Fresh mint leaves

1 Place the halved strawberries in a bowl with the melon balls. Peel the oranges and break into segments, then cut them in half or chop them roughly, depending on size. Add the oranges to the other fruit with any juices, adding extra orange juice if necessary. The fruit will usually create their own juice, especially if the melon is ripe.

2 Leave to stand for 30 minutes. Serve the fruit salad at room temperature, decorated with the fresh mint leaves.

pineapple with apricots and berries

AN UNUSUAL COMBINATION OF FRESH AND DRIED FRUITS. **SERVES 4**

½ cup (125 mL) dried apricots, soaked if necessary
1 large ripe pineapple
1 cup (250 mL) raspberries
1 cup (250 mL) blueberries
Sugar or honey to taste
Sprig of fresh mint, to garnish

1 Chop the apricots roughly. Cut the pineapple in half lengthwise if you wish to use it for serving, and cut away the flesh to leave a firm shell. Alternatively, peel the pineapple, core it, and dice the flesh into large chunks.

2 Mix the prepared pineapple with the apricots, raspberries, and blueberries, adding sugar as necessary, or drizzle with honey, then arrange the fruit in the prepared shell or on a serving dish. Chill lightly and garnish with mint before serving.

fig and pecan pie

FIGS ADD AN EXTRA TEXTURE, WITHOUT MAKING THE PIE TOO SWEET. **SERVES 8**

PASTRY

½ cup (125 mL) butter

1½ cups (375 mL) whole-wheat flour

Pinch of salt

Warm water

FILLING

½ cup (125 mL) unsalted butter

⅓ cup (90 mL) light brown sugar

½ cup (125 mL) honey

2 tsp (10 mL) vanilla extract

1 Tbsp (15 mL) coffee extract or extra-strong espresso coffee, cooled

¼ cup (60 mL) whiskey or orange juice

1 cup (250 mL) fresh figs, chopped

2 cups (500 mL) pecan halves

1 Preheat the oven to 375°F (190°C). Prepare the pastry by blending the butter into the flour and salt. Add sufficient warm water to make a firm dough, then roll out and use to line a 10-in (25-cm), loose-bottomed flan pan. Chill in the refrigerator while preparing the filling.

2 Cream the butter and sugar together until pale and creamy, then beat in the honey and vanilla. Add the coffee flavoring and the whiskey; beat in the figs and half the pecans, chopped. The mixture will appear to curdle, but don't worry!

3 Place the pastry pan on a cookie sheet, then spread the pastry with the filling. Arrange the remaining pecans on top of the pie. Bake in the preheated oven for 40 minutes. The filling will bubble up through the nuts during cooking, giving them a crunchy coating. Serve the pie warm or cold, with ice cream or yogurt.

pineapple oat meringues

THESE MERINGUES ARE NOT TOO SWEET AND HAVE A WONDERFUL COMBINATION OF FLAVORS. **SERVES 4**

2 Tbsp (25 mL) oats

4 slices fresh pineapple, cored

⅓ cup (90 mL) raisins

2 large egg whites

½ cup (125 mL) icing sugar

1 Preheat the oven to 375°F (190°C). Toast the oats until golden brown, either in a hot dry skillet or under a preheated broiler. Leave to cool.

2 Arrange the pineapple slices in individual ovenproof dishes and fill the centers with raisins. Whisk the egg whites to stiff peaks, then gradually whisk in the sugar. Fold in the toasted oatmeal, then spoon the mixture over the pineapple in the dishes, covering the fruit completely.

3 Bake in the preheated oven for 5 to 8 minutes, until set and lightly browned. Serve immediately.

mincemeat and apple tart

THE APPLES IN THE TART ADD LIGHTNESS TO THE RICH MINCEMEAT. **SERVES 6**

PASTRY

⅓ **cup (90 mL) butter**

1 cup (250 mL) whole-wheat flour

Grated rind and juice of 1 orange

1 to 2 medium baking apples, cored and sliced

Juice of 1 lemon

2 cups (500 mL) mincemeat

2 Tbsp (25 mL) honey

1 Preheat the oven to 375°F (190°C). Blend the butter into the flour, then stir in the orange rind. Bind the pastry with the orange juice, then roll it out and line an 8-in (20-cm) cake or flan pan. Toss the apples with the lemon juice.

2 Spread the mincemeat evenly in the pastry tin and arrange the sliced apples around the edge. Bake the tart in the preheated oven for 30 to 35 minutes.

3 Brush the apples carefully with honey as soon as the tart is removed from the oven, then leave to cool slightly before serving.

summer fruit upside-down trifle

USE FLAVORED YOGURT, IF YOU PREFER. **SERVES 6 TO 8**

2 lb (900 g) berries, fresh or frozen
1 cup (250 mL) light brown sugar
¼ cup (60 mL) butter
1½ cups (375 mL) crushed graham crackers
⅔ cup (150 mL) whole almonds, finely chopped
1 cup (250 mL) plain yogurt

1 Cook the berries with the sugar over low heat until they just start to burst. Allow the berries to cool, then strain off ½ cup (100 mL) syrup and set aside to cool. Melt the butter, stir in the graham cracker crumbs and almonds, and mix well. Set aside. Mix the cooled syrup with the yogurt.

2 Place the berries in the bottom of a glass serving dish; top with the flavored yogurt. Make a thick layer of the crumbs over the trifle, then chill for at least 30 minutes before serving.

spiced berry pudding

A FRESH FRUITY ALTERNATIVE TO HEAVY WINTER PUDDINGS. **SERVES 8**

1½ lb (700 g) mixed berries, fresh or frozen

¾ cup (175 mL) light brown sugar

1 tsp (5 mL) ground cinnamon

1 small fruit loaf, unsliced

1 Cook the berries with the sugar and cinnamon until they start to burst, then remove from the heat and set to one side.

2 Remove the crusts from the bread and cut it into ¼-in (5-mm) slices. Arrange the slices in a suitable pudding mold, cutting them so that they fit the mold neatly. Remove the bread and dip it, on both sides, in the fruit juices, then return it to the mold. Add the berries, removing them from the pot with a slotted spoon. Add sufficient juice to almost cover the berries (the bread will absorb a little more juice), then cover the pudding with more bread, dipping the slices into the juices.

3 Cover the pudding with a plate or saucer that will just sit on top of the bread, and place some heavy weights or cans on the plate. Allow the pudding to cool, then chill it for at least 6 hours or overnight.

4 To serve, carefully turn the pudding out onto a serving plate; if it has been well weighted and properly chilled, it should turn out easily and keep its shape. Serve with any remaining juices and yogurt or cream.

tangerine and cream cheese pancakes

OTHER FRUITS SUCH AS PEARS AND PEACHES ALSO WORK VERY WELL. **MAKES 8, SERVES 4**

FILLING

½ cup (125 mL) low-fat cream cheese

1 Tbsp (15 mL) light brown sugar

½ cup (125 mL) sour cream

4 tangerines or clementines, broken into segments

BATTER

1 large egg

1¼ cups (300 mL) milk

1 cup (250 mL) whole-wheat flour

Sunflower oil

1 Beat the cream cheese with the sugar, then blend in the sour cream. Set the filling to one side. Cut the tangerine segments in half if they are very big.

2 Preheat the oven to 375°F (190°C). Blend the egg and milk in a blender or food processor, then add the flour with the motor running. Blend to a smooth batter.

3 Heat a non-stick skillet until hot, then brush the bottom lightly with oil. Pour a little of the batter into the pan and cook quickly for about 1½ minutes, then turn or flip the pancake over and cook the second side. Stack the cooked pancakes, interleaved in paper towels or wax paper, until all the batter is used.

4 Divide the cream cheese mixture among the pancakes, spreading it evenly, then top with the tangerine segments. Roll up the pancakes, or fold them into quarters, and arrange in a large, ovenproof dish. Bake for 10 to 15 minutes in the preheated oven, just until heated through. Serve immediately while still hot.

prune and brandy mousse

A PRUNE PURÉE COMBINED WITH CREAM AND EGG WHITES TO MAKE A LIGHT MOUSSE. THIS RECIPE CONTAINS UNCOOKED EGG WHITE. **SERVES 6**

1 cup (250 mL) pitted prunes

½ cup (125 mL) cognac, or orange juice and cognac mixed

1 to 2 Tbsp (15 to 25 mL) light brown sugar

1 cup (250 mL) whipping cream

1 cup (250 mL) light cream

2 large egg whites

1 Purée the prunes with the cognac in a blender or food processor until smooth, then sweeten to taste.

2 Whip the creams together until soft and floppy – do not beat until stiff – then fold the cream into the prune purée. Whisk the egg whites until stiff; fold them into the prune cream. Turn into a serving bowl or 6 individual glasses and chill lightly before serving.

atholl brose

THIS TRADITIONAL SCOTTISH DISH OF OATMEAL, CREAM, AND HONEY IS UTTERLY ADDICTIVE. **SERVES 6 TO 8**

⅓ cup (90 mL) oatmeal

1½ cups (375 mL) whipping cream

½ cup (125 mL) light cream

2 to 3 Tbsp (15 to 25 mL) honey

¼ cup (60 mL) whiskey

Grated rind and juice of 1 medium orange

1 cup (250 mL) raspberries

1 Toast the oatmeal until golden brown, either in a hot, dry skillet or under a preheated broiler. Allow to cool.

2 Whisk the creams together until thick and floppy but not stiff. Add the honey, whiskey, and orange juice and whisk briefly until they are evenly incorporated into the cream. Fold in the oatmeal, orange rind, and raspberries, then turn into a serving bowl and chill lightly. Decorate with orange zest and mint before serving

orange and golden raisin rice pudding

USE ONLY THE ORANGE RIND; JUICE WILL CURDLE THE PUDDING. **SERVES 3 TO 4**

⅓ cup (90 mL) short-grain rice

⅓ cup (90 mL) golden raisins

1 tsp (5 mL) light brown sugar

Grated rind of 1 medium orange

2 cups (500 mL) milk

1 to 2 Tbsp (15 to 25 mL) margarine
   or butter

Nutmeg

1 Preheat the oven to 300°F (150°C). Place the rice and raisins in a lightly buttered casserole, and add the sugar and orange rind. Pour in the milk and stir to combine. Dot the top of the pudding with slivers of margarine or butter and sprinkle with nutmeg.

2 Bake the pudding slowly in the preheated oven for 2 hours. Serve hot or cold.

stuffed baked apples

DESPITE THEIR RELATIVELY LONG COOKING TIME, BAKED APPLES ARE AN EASY DELICIOUS WINTER DESSERT; JUST PUT IN THE OVEN TO COOK WHILE YOU EAT YOUR DINNER. **SERVES 4**

4 medium baking apples

½ cup (125 mL) dried figs, chopped

1 Tbsp (15 mL) golden raisins

3 Tbsp (45 mL) honey

Yogurt, custard, or cream to serve

1 Preheat the oven to 350°F (175°C). Carefully remove the cores from the apples, either with a corer or a small, sharp knife. Pierce the skin of each apple to prevent it from bursting during cooking, then place in a buttered ovenproof dish.

2 Mix the chopped figs with the raisins, then pack into the apples. Drizzle the honey over the apples, then pour half a cup of water into the bottom of the dish. Bake the apples in the preheated oven for about 45 minutes, until just tender — test them with the tip of a sharp knife. Do not overcook, or the apples will collapse. Serve hot with yogurt, custard, or cream.

danish apple cake

SERVE TOPPED WITH WHIPPED CREAM AND DUSTED WITH CHOCOLATE. **SERVES 4 TO 6**

3 cups (750 mL) fresh whole-wheat bread crumbs

⅓ cup (90 mL) Demerara sugar

⅓ cup (90 mL) butter

4 cups (1 L) baking apples, peeled, cored, and sliced

Grated rind and juice of 1 lemon

1 Mix the bread crumbs with the sugar. Melt the butter in a large skillet, add the crumb mixture and fry quickly until the crumbs are crisp, then set them to one side.

2 Cook the apples with the lemon rind and juice and as little water as possible, until soft. I usually cook apples in a microwave because no water is required. Allow to cool.

3 Turn half the apples into a glass dish, then make a layer of half the crumbs over the apples. Repeat the layers, finishing with the remaining crumbs. Allow the pudding to cool completely, then chill for at least 1 hour before serving.

soft fruits with lime mascarpone

SWEET FRUITS SERVED WITH A RICH AND WICKED LIME-
FLAVORED CREAM MIXED WITH TOASTED NUTS. **SERVES 4**

⅓ **cup (90 mL) hazelnuts or almonds**

4 medium ripe peaches

1 Tbsp (25 mL) lemon juice

2 cups (500 mL) raspberries

1 cup (250 mL) mascarpone cheese or crème fraîche

2 Tbsp (25 mL) thick plain yogurt

Grated rind and juice of 1 lime

1 Tbsp (15 mL) icing sugar

Lime juice, to serve

1 Toast the nuts until golden brown in a non-stick skillet or under a broiler, then leave to cool before chopping finely.

2 Cut the peaches in half and remove the stones, then toss the peaches quickly in the lemon juice to prevent discoloration. Arrange the peaches on individual plates with the fresh raspberries.

3 Beat the mascarpone until smooth, then add the yogurt, lime rind, and juice, and beat again. Add sugar to taste and fold in the chopped nuts. Serve with the prepared fruits, drizzled with lime juice.

5 Breads, cakes, and cookies

High-fiber baking is quite different from baking with refined white flour. Bran tends to absorb liquid and, as the whole-wheat kernel with all the bran is ground for whole-wheat flour, I find it necessary to add more liquid than I would with white flour. I notice it especially with cakes and quick breads.

Different flours always have different characteristics and liquid absorption rates, so even if you always use the same brand, be prepared to check a mixture and adjust the liquid if necessary. This particularly applies to bread making. It is easy to add more, but taking away is difficult, so always add the measured amount gradually. I like to bake with stone-ground or organic flours, both of which produce silky doughs. Again, the water absorption rate of these flours tends to be different from regular whole-wheat flour.

You may be able to find "fine" whole-wheat flour in your area. If so, use it for pastry, cakes and cookies, sauces, and batters. It is often labeled "for cakes and pastry" on the bag and has revolutionized high-fiber baking, producing lighter results. There is little point in sifting any whole-wheat flour, as you will simply remove the bran from it.

These baking recipes have all been selected for their fiber content, but that does not mean that they are suitable for eating all day long! The cakes and cookies are still high in calories and should be eaten as a treat rather than as a basic part of your diet. Homemade whole-wheat bread is far more filling than commercial bread, so you should require less of it.

LEFT HONEYED GINGER CAKE (SEE PAGE 208)

toasted hazelnut rye bread

THIS IS AN EXCELLENT LOAF, FULL OF NUTTY TASTE AND TEXTURE. **MAKES 1 LARGE LOAF**

- **3 cups (750 mL) whole-wheat flour**
- **2 cups (500 mL) rye flour**
- **2 tsp (10 mL) salt**
- **⅓ cup (90 mL) poppy seeds**
- **⅓ cup (90 mL) toasted hazelnuts, chopped**
- **1 packet active yeast**
- **3 Tbsp (45 mL) hazelnut or olive oil**
- **2 cups (500 mL) warm water**

1 Mix the flours, salt, poppy seeds, nuts, and yeast together in a large bowl. Add the oil and sufficient water to form a manageable dough. Turn onto a lightly floured surface and knead thoroughly for about 5 minutes, until the dough is smooth – it will not become as elastic as a pure wheat dough. Shape into a round loaf and place on a lightly oiled cookie sheet, then cover and leave in a warm place for about 1 hour, until the dough has almost doubled in size.

2 Preheat the oven to 425°F (220°C). Score the top of the loaf with a sharp knife, if wished, then bake for 40 minutes until the base of the loaf sounds hollow when tapped. Cool on a wire rack.

barley and rye bread

BARLEY FLOUR IS SLIGHTLY SWEET AND COMBINES WELL WITH THE MORE SOUR FLAVOR OF THE RYE.
MAKES 1 LOAF

- **1½ cups (375 mL) warm water**
- **2 cups (500 mL) whole-wheat flour**
- **2 packages active dry yeast**
- **1 cup (250 mL) barley flour**
- **1 cup (250 mL) rye flour**

1 Place the water in a large bowl; add 1 cup (250 mL) whole-wheat flour and 1 package of yeast. Blend to a smooth paste, then cover and leave in a warm place for 30 minutes, until full of bubbles.

2 Add the barley and rye flours to the ferment along with the salt and the remaining yeast. Gradually add the remaining whole-wheat flour, using as much as necessary to produce a workable dough. Turn out onto a lightly floured surface and knead thoroughly for about 10 minutes, until smooth. This dough will not become elastic.

3 Shape into a loaf and place in a large, greased loaf pan. Cover and leave in a warm place for about 1 hour, until well risen.

4 Preheat the oven to 425°F (220°C). Sprinkle a little flour over the loaf and bake for 35 to 40 minutes, until the loaf sounds hollow when tapped. Turn out and cool on a wire rack.

pumpkin and cheese bread

THE PUMPKIN PURÉE ADDS MOISTURE TO THE LOAF. **MAKES 1 LOAF**

- 2½ cups (750 mL) whole-wheat bread flour
- 1 tsp (5 mL) salt
- 1 package active dry yeast
- 1 Tbsp (15 mL) olive oil
- 1 cup (15 mL) thick pumpkin purée
- 1 cup (15 mL) warm water
- 1 cup (250 mL) grated Cheddar cheese

1 Place the flour and salt in a large bowl and stir in the yeast. Make a well in the center and add the oil and pumpkin purée, then mix to a manageable dough with the water. Turn onto a lightly floured surface and knead thoroughly for about 10 minutes until elastic. Return the dough to the bowl, cover, and leave in a warm place for about 1 hour, until doubled in size.

2 Punch down the dough, kneading it lightly to incorporate the grated cheese. Shape into a round and place on a lightly greased baking sheet, then cover the dough and leave for a further 40 minutes until well risen.

3 Preheat the oven to 425°F (220°C). Sprinkle a little whole-wheat flour over the loaf, then bake for 35 to 40 minutes. Cool on a wire rack.

pear and banana bread

OTHER FRUITS CAN BE USED, BUT THIS IS MY FAVORITE COMBINATION.

MAKES 1 LARGE LOAF

3 cups (375 mL) whole-wheat flour

¾ cup (175 mL) bran

1½ tsp (7 mL) baking soda

1 tsp (5 mL) baking powder

Pinch of salt

⅓ cup (90 mL) light brown sugar

¼ cup (60 mL) dried pears, chopped

¾ cup (175 mL) mashed ripe banana

1 large egg, beaten

2 cups (500 mL) buttermilk

1 Preheat the oven to 350°F (175°C) and lightly grease a large loaf pan.

2 Place all the dry ingredients in a bowl and mix together, adding the chopped pears. Make a well in the center and add the banana. Beat the egg into the buttermilk, pour it over the banana and mix together briefly – this is like a soda bread and should not be overworked, or it will not rise.

3 Spoon the mixture into the prepared pan, then bake in the preheated oven for 1 hour, or until a toothpick inserted into the loaf comes out clean. Cool in the pan for a few minutes, then turn out onto a wire rack to cool completely.

spiced orange breakfast bread

THIS LOAF, BASED ON SWEDISH LIMPA BREAD, IS SPICED AND FLAVORED WITH ORANGE AND MAKES A WONDERFUL BREAKFAST BREAD. **MAKES 1 LOAF**

1 cup (250 mL) water

1 tsp (5 mL) caraway seeds

1 Tbsp (15 mL) fennel seeds

1 Tbsp (15 mL) liquid honey

Grated rind of 1 orange

2 cups (500 mL) rye flour

2 cups (500 mL) whole-wheat bread flour

1 tsp (5 mL) salt

1 package active dry yeast

2 Tbsp (250 mL) olive oil

1 Heat the water with the spices, honey, and orange rind until the honey has dissolved and the mixture is hot but not boiling. Leave to cool until tepid.

2 Mix all the dry ingredients together in a large bowl and add the oil. Pour the spiced water into the flours and mix to a manageable dough, adding the juice from the orange if the mixture is too dry. Knead thoroughly until the dough is smooth – this combination of flours will not produce a soft and really stretchy dough. Return the dough to the bowl, cover, and leave in a warm place for 1 hour, until well risen.

3 Punch the dough down, kneading it lightly, then shape into a loaf and place in a greased loaf pan. Cover and leave for a further 40 minutes.

4 Preheat the oven to 425°F (220°C). Bake the loaf for 45 minutes, remove from the pan and cool on a wire rack.

light rye sourdough

I CALL THIS A LIGHT RYE SOURDOUGH BECAUSE MOST RYE BREADS ARE VERY HEAVY. **MAKES 1 LOAF**

2 cups (500 mL) tepid milk

3½ cups (875 mL) whole-wheat bread flour

2 packages active dry yeast

2½ cups (625 mL) rye flour

1 Tbsp (15 mL) salt

1 Place the milk in a large bowl, then stir in 2 cups (500 mL) of whole-wheat bread flour and 1 package of yeast. Blend until smooth, cover and leave in a warm place for 14 hours – this is best done overnight.

2 Mix the rye flour, salt, and remaining yeast into the mixture and add as much of the whole-wheat bread flour as necessary to give a manageable dough. Turn onto a lightly floured surface and knead thoroughly until smooth – the dough will not become very elastic.

3 Shape into a round loaf and place on a floured baking sheet, or shape and place in a greased loaf pan. Cover and leave in a warm place for about 1 hour, until well risen.

4 Preheat the oven to 425°F (220°C). Bake the loaf for 20 minutes, then reduce the temperature to 375°F (190°C) and continue cooking for a further 20 minutes. Turn the loaf out onto a wire rack to cool.

soda bread

THE SECRET OF A LIGHT SODA BREAD LOAF IS TO NOT OVERMIX. THE DOUGH SHOULD JUST BE GATHERED TOGETHER AND NEVER KNEADED. **MAKES 1 LOAF**

3 cups (750 mL) whole-wheat flour

¾ cup (175 mL) bran

Pinch of salt

2 tsp (10 mL) baking soda

1 Tbsp (15 mL) light brown sugar

2 cups (500 mL) buttermilk

1 Preheat the oven to 400°F (200°C) and lightly grease a deep 7-in (18-cm) round cake pan.

2 Mix together all the dry ingredients then add the buttermilk and mix quickly with a broad-bladed knife. Turn the dough out of the bowl and bring it together gently with your hands – do not actually knead the dough or overwork it, as this will make the bread heavy. Form into a round and place in the prepared cake pan.

3 Bake the soda bread in the preheated oven for 40 minutes, then turn out and cool on a wire rack. Eat the soda bread on the day it is baked.

potato griddle scones

WARM POTATO MAKES LIGHTER SCONES, SO HEAT THE POTATO THROUGH (A MICROWAVE WORKS WELL)
BEFORE MIXING THE DOUGH. **MAKES ABOUT 20**

1½ cups (375 mL) mashed potato

½ tsp (2 mL) salt

1 Tbsp (15 mL) margarine or butter

½ cup (125 mL) whole-wheat flour

1 Mix the mashed potato with the salt and margarine, then add sufficient flour to produce a stiff dough. Knead lightly on a floured surface and roll out to a ¼ in (0.5 cm) thickness. Cut into 2-in (5-cm) rounds.

2 Preheat a griddle or heavy skillet, then cook the scones for 4 to 5 minutes, until lightly browned on both sides. Turn once during cooking. Serve spread with butter or margarine.

nutbread loaves

THESE ARE COMMONLY NAMED AFTER DORIS GRANT, A WHOLEFOOD CAMPAIGNER WHO PERFECTED A LOAF
PREPARED WITH NO KNEADING. IT WORKS WELL DESPITE BREAKING BAKING CONVENTIONS! **MAKES 3 LOAVES**

8 cups (2 L) stone-ground whole-wheat flour

2 tsp (10 mL) salt

2 packages active dry yeast

1 cup (250 mL) chopped walnuts, pumpkin, and sunflower seeds, mixed

2 tsp (10 mL) light molasses

5 cups (1.25 L) warm water

1 Lightly grease three large loaf pans. Have the flour, mixing bowl, and loaf pans warm, especially in cold weather – this is a quick loaf to mix and cook, but because of the yeast it does require warmth. You can warm them by placing the flour in the mixing bowl and place in a warm oven (200°F/105°C) with the loaf pans for 20 minutes.

2 Place the flour, salt, yeast, nuts, and seeds in a large, warm bowl and mix well. Add the molasses to the warm water and whisk until blended. Make a large well in the center of the flour, add the water. Mix with a wooden spoon, scraping the flour from the edge of the bowl. Continue mixing until a dough is formed, then mix with your hands until it leaves the sides of the bowl. The dough should be sticky but not wet. Preheat the oven to 400°F (200°C).

3 Turn onto a very lightly floured surface and divide into 3 – the dough will be much softer and stickier than a regular dough. Shape roughly and place in the loaf pans. Cover, and leave in a warm place for 30 to 40 minutes, until the dough has risen slightly. Bake the loaves in the hot oven for 35 to 40 minutes, until the bases sound hollow when tapped. Cool on a wire rack.

quick onion and nut loaf

THIS IS A GREAT LOAF TO SERVE WITH SOUPS AND CHOWDERS. **MAKES 1 LOAF**

2 cups (500 mL) whole-wheat flour

2 tsp (10 mL) baking powder

½ tsp (2 mL) salt

1 Tbsp (15 mL) margarine or butter

2 Tbsp (25 mL) chopped parsley

½ cup (125 mL) coarsely grated onion

½ cup (125 mL) pecan nuts, chopped

1 large egg, beaten

1 tsp (5 mL) Dijon mustard

1 cup (250 mL) milk

1 Preheat the oven to 375°F (190°C) and lightly grease a small loaf pan.

2 Mix all the dry ingredients together in a bowl, then blend in the margarine. Stir in the parsley, onion, and pecans. Beat the egg with the mustard and add to the milk. Pour the liquid into the flour and mix to a stiff, wet batter. Transfer the mixture into the prepared loaf pan – it will almost fill it – and smooth the top.

3 Bake in the preheated oven for 45 to 50 minutes, until set and lightly browned. Cool for a few minutes in the pan, then turn out onto a wire rack to cool.

wild rice quick bread

THIS MAKES A DELICIOUSLY MOIST LOAF THAT IS ESPECIALLY GOOD WITH GOAT CHEESE. **MAKES 1 LOAF**

½ cup (125 mL) wild rice

2½ cups (375 mL) water

2 Tbsp (25 mL) molasses

2 Tbsp (25 mL) olive oil

1¼ cups (300 mL) whole-wheat flour

2 tsp (10 mL) baking powder

½ tsp (5 mL) salt

2 Tbsp (25 mL) chopped fresh chives

½ cup (125 mL) walnut pieces, chopped

1 large egg, beaten

1 Bring the rice to a boil in the water, then cover the pot and cook for 45 minutes, until the rice has nearly absorbed the water and the grains have split. Stir the molasses into the rice, leave to cool for 30 minutes.

2 Preheat the oven to 325°F (160°C) and lightly grease a large loaf pan. Add the oil to the rice, then beat in the flour, baking powder, salt, chives, and walnuts. Beat the egg into the mixture and then pour it into the prepared loaf pan. Smooth the top and bake in the preheated oven for 1 hour, or until a toothpick inserted into the loaf comes out clean.

3 Loosen the loaf in the pan, then turn it out carefully onto a wire rack to cool. Serve with soft goat cheese, if you like.

malted grain bread

A GREAT BREAD FOR BEGINNERS, THE METHOD ENCOURAGES YOU TO KEEP ADDING FLOUR UNTIL YOU HAVE THE CORRECT TEXTURE. **MAKES 2 LARGE LOAVES**

4 cups (1 L) tepid water

8 to 8½ cups (2 to 2.1 L) malted grain flour

2 packages active dry yeast

1 Tbsp (15 mL) salt

¼ cup (60 mL) olive oil (optional)

1 Place the water in a large bowl – use the mixer bowl if you intend to knead the dough by machine. Sprinkle 3 cups (750 mL) flour on the water with the yeast, then mix to a smooth creamy paste. Cover and leave in a warm place for about 30 minutes, until very frothy.

2 Add the salt and oil to the yeast, then work in the remaining flour until the dough is easily manageable and does not stick to the work surface. Knead thoroughly until smooth and fairly elastic, then halve the dough and shape into loaves. Place the loaves on floured baking sheets or in lightly greased loaf pans. The dough should fill the loaf pans just over half. Cover and leave in a warm place for about 40 minutes, until almost doubled in size. Preheat the oven to 425°F (220°C). Sprinkle a little extra flour over the loaves, then bake in the preheated oven for 45 minutes, or until the base sounds hollow when tapped. Cool on a wire rack.

bran bread

THE ALL-BRAN® CEREAL ADDS BRAN TO THE RECIPE AND MAINTAINS A LIGHT, APPEALING COLOR.

MAKES 1 LOAF

- 2½ cups (625 mL) whole-wheat bread flour
- 1 tsp (5 mL) salt
- ½ cup (125 mL) All-Bran® cereal
- 1 package active dry yeast
- 2 Tbsp (25 mL) oil
- 1½ cups (375 mL) warm milk and water, mixed

1 Place the flour, salt, and All-Bran® in a bowl; stir in the yeast. Add the oil, then add sufficient of the milk and water mixture to give a soft, manageable dough. You may find that you need a little extra liquid – the All-Bran® will absorb quite a lot.

2 Turn onto a floured surface and knead thoroughly for about 10 minutes until smooth. Shape into a round loaf and place on a lightly greased baking sheet. Cover and leave in a warm place for about 1 hour, until well risen.

3 Preheat the oven to 425°F (220°C). Press a little extra All-Bran® lightly into the top of the loaf, then bake for 30 to 35 minutes. The base of the loaf should sound hollow. Transfer to a wire rack to cool.

whole-wheat cheese rolls

I LIKE TO ADD A LITTLE WHITE FLOUR TO THIS MIXTURE, WHICH SHOULD BE SOFT AND SILKY. **MAKES 8**

¼ cup (60 mL) lard, margarine or
    butter

2½ cups (375 mL) whole-wheat bread
    flour

1 cup (250 mL) all-purpose flour

1 tsp (5 mL) salt

1 package active dry yeast

1 cup (250 mL) warm milk and water,
    mixed

¼ cup (60 mL) sunflower seeds

½ cup (125 mL) grated Cheddar
    cheese

1 Blend the lard into the flours and salt in a large bowl. Stir in the yeast and mix to a manageable dough with the warm liquid, adding a little extra if necessary. Knead thoroughly on a lightly floured surface until soft and elastic, return the dough to the bowl, cover, and leave in a warm place for about 1½ hours, until doubled in size.

2 Punch the dough down, kneading it lightly to incorporate the sunflower seeds. Shape into 8 rolls, then roll out until ½ in (1.25 cm) thick. Place the rolls on lightly greased baking sheets, cover and leave in a warm place for a further 30 to 40 minutes.

3 Preheat the oven to 400°F (200°C). Sprinkle the cheese over the rolls and bake in the preheated oven for 15 to 20 minutes. Transfer to a wire rack to cool.

chapatis

DO NOT OVERCOOK THESE INDIAN FLATBREADS OR THEY WILL BECOME HARD. **MAKES 6**

1 Tbsp (15 mL) butter

1 cup (250 mL) whole-wheat flour

Good pinch of salt

About ⅔ cup (150 mL) warm water

1 Blend the butter into the flour and salt, then mix to a soft dough with the water – add the liquid gradually, as the amount required depends on the flour being used. Turn onto a floured surface and knead until smooth and pliable. Return the dough to the bowl, cover and leave in a warm place for 30 minutes.

2 Divide the dough into 6 balls. Dip in a little extra flour, then roll them out into circles approximately 6 in (15 cm) in diameter.

3 Heat a griddle or a non-stick skillet until evenly hot, and cook the chapatis for about 30 seconds on each side – turn them when brown spots start to appear on the surface. Keep the cooked breads warm in a clean dish towel until all the chapatis are cooked. Serve warm.

creamed corn cornbread

A SWEET, YET SAVORY, BREAD, THIS MAKES A GOOD LUNCHTIME
SNACK OR CAN BE USED IN PLACE OF POTATOES, RICE, OR PASTA WITH
A MEAL. **MAKES 1 LARGE LOAF**

1 cup (250 mL) yellow cornmeal

1 cup (250 mL) whole-wheat flour

2½ tsp (12 mL) baking powder

1 Tbsp (15 mL) light brown sugar

2 Tbsp (25 mL) dried sweet bell pepper flakes or
   1 Tbsp (15 mL) dried chile flakes (optional)

½ tsp (2 mL) salt

3 large eggs, separated

15-oz (425-g) can creamed corn

⅔ cup (150 mL) whipping cream

½ cup (125 mL) butter, melted

1 Preheat the oven to 375°F (190°C) and lightly grease a deep
8- or 9-in (20- or 23-cm) round cake pan.

2 Mix all the dry ingredients together in a large bowl. Separate
the eggs and combine the yolks with the remaining
ingredients. Whisk the egg whites until stiff. Beat the corn mixture
into the dry ingredients until well mixed, then fold the egg white
through the mixture until evenly blended. Pour into the prepared
cake pan and bake in the preheated oven for 45 minutes, until
lightly browned and set.

3 Carefully remove the cornbread from the pan and allow it to
cool slightly before serving warm. It may also be served hot,
straight from the oven, as part of a meal.

molasses cornbread

I PREFER THIS RECIPE TO A CORNBREAD MADE WITH BAKING POWDER. **MAKES 1 LOAF**

¼ cup (60 mL) light molasses

¼ cup (60 mL) olive oil

1¼ cups (300 mL) milk

2½ cups (625 mL) whole-wheat flour

2 cups (500 mL) cornmeal

2 tsp (10 mL) salt

2 packages active dry yeast

1 Heat the molasses, oil, and milk together until the molasses has blended with the other ingredients. Remove from the heat and allow to cool. Mix the flour, cornmeal, salt, and yeast together in a large bowl and make a well in the center. Pour in the cooled molasses mixture and mix to a manageable dough.

2 Knead thoroughly until smooth – this dough will not become elastic. Shape into a loaf and place in a large, greased loaf pan, then cover and leave in a warm place for 1½ hours, until risen just above the top of the loaf pan.

3 Preheat the oven to 425°F (220°C) while the dough is rising. Sprinkle a little extra cornmeal over the loaf and bake in the preheated oven for 35 minutes, or until the base of the loaf sounds hollow when tapped. Cool on a wire rack.

whole-wheat sandwich loaf

THIS IS A GREAT EVERYDAY BREAD THAT CHILDREN WILL LOVE. **MAKES 2 LARGE LOAVES**

6 cups (1.5 L) whole-wheat bread
   flour

2 cups (500 mL) white bread flour

1 Tbsp (15 mL) salt

2 packages active dry yeast

¼ cup (60 mL) olive oil

About 4 cups (1 L) tepid water

1 Place all the dry ingredients in a large bowl and mix in the yeast. Add the oil and most of the water, then mix to a workable dough, adding the remaining water if necessary. Turn out onto a floured surface and knead thoroughly for about 10 minutes until smooth and fairly elastic.

2 Shape the dough into 2 loaves. Place the loaves either on floured baking sheets or in lightly greased loaf pans. The dough should fill the loaf pans just over half. Cover and leave in a warm place for about 40 minutes, until well-risen and almost doubled in size.

3 Preheat the oven to 425°F (220°C). Sprinkle a little extra flour over the loaves, then bake in the preheated oven for 45 minutes, or until the bases sound hollow when tapped. Cool on a wire rack.

whole-wheat morning rolls

THIS OVERNIGHT DOUGH MAKES CREAMY, SOFT ROLLS FOR BREAKFAST. **MAKES 18**

OVERNIGHT

2½ cups (625 mL) warm water

3 cups (750 mL) whole-wheat
   bread flour

1 Tbsp (15 mL) salt

1 package active dry yeast

MORNING

1 package active dry yeast

¾ cup (175 mL) warm water

3½ cups (875 mL) whole-wheat
   bread flour

¼ cup (60 mL) margarine or butter

1 tsp (5 mL) light brown sugar

1 Place the water for the overnight dough in a large bowl. Add the flour, salt, and yeast and mix lightly – do not beat or knead. Cover and leave overnight at room temperature.

2 In the morning, add all the remaining ingredients to the bowl and mix to a manageable dough; the margarine will be incorporated during the mixing. Turn out onto a floured surface and knead well for about 10 minutes until the dough has become smooth and elastic.

3 Shape the dough into 18 rolls. Place them on lightly greased baking sheets, just touching. Cover and leave in a warm place for 30 minutes to rise.

4 Preheat the oven to 425°F (220°C). Bake the rolls for about 20 minutes. The bases will sound hollow when tapped, but the tops of the rolls will only brown slightly and remain soft. Cool on a wire rack.

golden raisin scones

A DELICIOUS TREAT FOR AFTERNOON TEA! **MAKES 12**

2 Tbsp (25 mL) butter

3 cup (750 mL) whole-wheat flour

2 tsp (10 mL) baking powder

¼ cup (90 mL) light brown sugar

½ cup (125 mL) golden raisins

1 large egg, beaten

About ⅔ cup (150 mL) milk

1 Preheat the oven to 425°F (220°C) and lightly grease a large baking sheet. Blend the butter into the flour and baking powder, then stir in the sugar and raisins. Make a well in the center and pour in the beaten egg. Mix to a soft dough with the milk.

2 Knead the dough on a lightly floured surface until smooth, then roll out until ½-in (1.25-cm) thick. Cut out with a 2-in (5-cm) cutter and place the scones on the prepared baking sheet.

3 Bake for 10 minutes in the preheated oven, then cool slightly on a wire rack before serving.

cheese and walnut scone rounds

THESE SCONES ARE A PERFECT ACCOMPANIMENT TO SOUPS AND STEWS. **SERVES 4 TO 8**

½ cup (125 mL) butter

2 cups (500 mL) whole-wheat flour

2 tsp (10 mL) baking powder

Pinch of salt

½ cup (125 mL) walnuts, chopped

1 cup (125 mL) grated Cheddar
   cheese

1 large egg, beaten

½ cup (125 mL) milk

1 Preheat the oven to 425°F (220°C) and lightly oil a cookie sheet.

2 Blend the butter into the flour, baking powder, and salt, and stir in the nuts and cheese. Beat the egg with the milk and use to mix to a soft but manageable dough.

3 Turn onto a lightly floured surface then knead lightly until smooth. Shape the dough into a round about 1 in (2.5 cm) thick, and score 8 portions. Bake on the cookie sheet for 20 to 25 minutes. Cool for at least 10 minutes.

whole-wheat drop scones

ALSO KNOWN AS SCOTCH PANCAKES, THESE ARE QUICK TO MAKE AND DELICIOUS TO EAT. **MAKES ABOUT 12**

⅔ cup (150 mL) whole-wheat flour

1 tsp (5 mL) baking powder

Pinch of salt

1 large egg, beaten

⅔ cup (150 mL) milk, or milk and
   water mixed

1 Mix the flour, baking powder, and salt together in a bowl and make a well in the center. Beat the egg with the milk, add it to the flour, and beat to a smooth, thick batter.

2 Heat a heavy skillet until evenly hot then drop tablespoonfuls of the mixture onto the surface, allowing room for them to spread slightly. Turn the scones after a minute or so, when bubbles begin to rise to the surface. Cook for a further 1 to 2 minutes then serve.

sticky buns

EVEN WHEN MADE THE HIGH-FIBER WAY, THESE YEASTED BUNS ARE UTTERLY DECADENT AND TOTALLY DELICIOUS. **MAKES 8**

2 cups (500 mL) whole-wheat bread flour

1 package active dry yeast

⅔ cup (150 mL) warm milk

1 Tbsp (15 mL) margarine or butter

½ tsp (5 mL) salt

1 egg, beaten

FILLING

¼ cup (60 mL) butter or margarine

¼ cup (60 mL) light brown sugar

2 tsp (10 mL) pumpkin pie spice *

⅔ cup (150 mL) currants or raisins

* (½ tsp (2 mL) cinnamon, ½ tsp (2 mL) ground ginger, ½ tsp (2 mL) nutmeg, ¼ tsp (1 mL) allspice, ¼ tsp (1 mL) mace, ⅛ tsp (.5 mL) ground cloves)

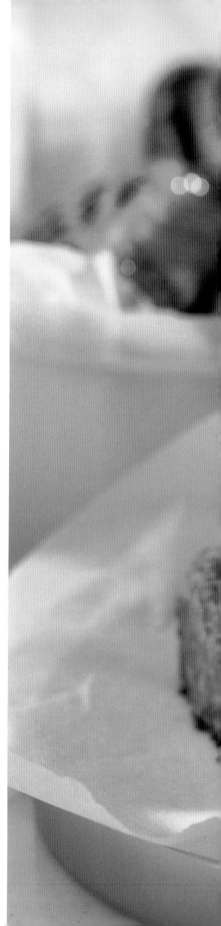

1 Place ¼ cup (60 mL) flour in a small bowl with the yeast and add the warm milk. Mix to a smooth paste, cover and leave in a warm place for 25 to 30 minutes until frothy. Blend the margarine into the remaining flour and salt in a large bowl; make a well in the center. Beat the egg and pour it into the dry ingredients. Add the yeast and mix into a manageable dough. Knead thoroughly until smooth and elastic, then return the dough to the bowl. Cover and leave in a warm place for about 1½ hours, until doubled in size.

2 Lightly grease a deep 8-in (20-cm), round baking pan. Melt together the butter, sugar, and spice for the filling and allow to cool slightly. Pour half the mixture into the pan and spread evenly over the base. Punch the dough down by kneading lightly, then roll out into a rectangle about 12 x 8 in (30 x 20 cm). Spread the remaining syrup over the dough, then sprinkle with the currants. Roll up, trim the ends, then cut the dough into 8 pieces. Place them in the pan with the joins towards the center. Cover and leave in a warm place for a further 40 minutes.

3 Preheat the oven to 375°F (190°C). Bake the buns in the preheated oven for about 25 minutes. Leave in the tin to cool for 2 to 3 minutes before turning out onto a wire rack to cool.

spiced fruit buns

COOK THE BUNS SPACED OUT ON A BAKING TRAY OR IN MUFFIN PANS. **MAKES 15 TO 18**

½ cup (125 mL) butter or margarine

2 cups (500 mL) whole-wheat flour

1 heaping tsp (5 mL) baking powder

Pinch of salt

1 to 2 tsp (5 to 10 mL) pumpkin pie
spice (see p. 200)

1 cup (250 mL) dried mixed fruit,
such as golden raisins, currants,
cranberries

1 egg, beaten

⅓ cup (150 mL) milk

1 Preheat the oven to 400°F (200°C) and lightly grease some muffin pans. Blend the butter into the flour, baking powder, salt, and spice in a bowl until the mixture resembles fine bread crumbs. Stir in the fruit, add the beaten egg and the milk, and mix to a stiff dough.

2 Place spoonfuls of mixture in the prepared muffin pans and bake in the preheated oven for 20 to 25 minutes. Cool on a wire rack.

whole-wheat honey and pecan bread

THIS IS A QUICK-MIX YEASTED LOAF, BEST SERVED SLICED AND BUTTERED WITH JAM OR HONEY.

3 cups (750 mL) whole-wheat
bread flour

1 cup (250 mL) wheat germ

½ tsp (2 mL) salt

1 package active dry yeast

¾ cup (175 mL) raisins

¾ cup (175 mL) toasted
hazelnuts, chopped

2 Tbsp (25 mL) sunflower oil

¼ cup (60 mL) honey

1 to 1½ cups (250 to 375 mL)
warm water

1 Mix all the dry ingredients together in a large bowl and make a well in the center. Add the oil, honey, and 1 cup (250 mL) warm water, then mix to form a manageable dough, adding extra water as necessary. Do not add too much water or the dough will become very sticky.

2 Turn the dough out onto a lightly floured surface and knead thoroughly until smooth. Shape into a loaf and place in a large, greased loaf pan – the dough should fill to just over half. Cover and leave in a warm place for about 1 hour, until well risen.

3 Preheat the oven to 425°F (220°C). Bake the loaf for 10 minutes, then reduce the temperature to 400°F (200°C) and continue cooking for a further 30 to 35 minutes. Cool on a wire rack. Serve sliced and buttered.

quick bran teabread

THE MIXTURE IS VERY WET WHEN IT GOES INTO THE OVEN AND IS USUALLY FROTHING. DON'T WORRY – THIS IS HOW IT SHOULD BE. **MAKES 1 LOAF**

1 cup (250 mL) mixed dried fruit

1 cup (250 mL) cold tea

½ cup (125 mL) light brown sugar

¼ cup (60 mL) margarine

¼ cup (60 mL) orange marmalade

1 cup (250 mL) whole-wheat flour

1 tsp (5 mL) baking powder

1 tsp (5 mL) baking soda

1 tsp (5 mL) pumpkin pie spice (see p. 200)

Pinch of salt

1 cup (250 mL) All-Bran® cereal

1 egg, beaten

1 Preheat the oven to 350°F (175°C) and lightly grease a large loaf pan. Place the dried fruit, tea, sugar, margarine, and marmalade in a saucepan and heat gently until the sugar has dissolved and the margarine melted, then leave to cool.

2 Mix the dry ingredients together in a large bowl and make a well in the center. Beat the egg and add it to the fruit mixture, then pour into the dry ingredients and mix thoroughly and quickly. Pour immediately into the prepared loaf pan. Bake in the preheated oven for 50 to 60 minutes, until a toothpick inserted into the loaf comes out clean.

3 Cool the teabread on a wire rack. Serve sliced and lightly buttered.

banana cornmeal muffins

DELICIOUSLY LIGHT MUFFINS, UNDERSCORED WITH THE FLAVOR OF GINGER. **MAKES 12**

1 cup (250 mL) whole-wheat flour

½ cup (125 mL) cornmeal

½ cup (125 mL) light brown sugar

1½ tsp (7 mL) baking powder

½ tsp (2 mL) baking soda

Pinch of salt

1 tsp (5 mL) ground ginger

¾ cup (175 mL) roughly mashed ripe banana (3 medium)

2 large eggs, beaten

1 cup (250 mL) sour cream

1 Tbsp (15 mL) margarine or butter, melted, or oil

1 Preheat the oven to 350°F (175°C) and line 12 muffin cups with paper cups.

2 Mix all the dry ingredients together in a bowl and add the bananas. Beat the eggs with the sour cream and add the melted margarine. Pour into the dry ingredients and work quickly until the mixture is combined together – do not beat.

3 Divide the mixture between the muffin cups, then bake in the preheated oven for 25 minutes, until a toothpick inserted into the muffins comes out clean. Cool briefly on a wire rack. Serve warm.

fig cake

THE ORANGE JUICE PREVENTS THE MIXTURE FROM BECOMING TOO SWEET. **MAKES 1 CAKE**

1½ cups (375 mL) roughly chopped dried figs

Grated rind and juice of 1 medium orange

¾ stick (175 mL) butter

2 cups (500 mL) whole-wheat flour

Pinch of salt

⅔ cup (150 mL) soft brown sugar

1 large egg, beaten

1 Place the figs, orange rind, and juice in a pan and cook slowly for 10 to 15 minutes until soft. Mash together gently with a wooden spoon then set aside.

2 Blend the butter into the flour, salt, and sugar. Add the egg and sufficient water to mix to a manageable dough. Roll out half the mixture and press into the bottom of an 8-in (20-cm) baking pan with a loose bottom, then spread with the figs. Roll the remaining dough into a circle just a little smaller than the tin, then place over the figs and press down firmly sealing the two crusts together. Chill the fig cake while preheating the oven.

3 Preheat the oven to 375°F (190°C). Bake the cake for 30 minutes, or until the dough is set. Mark into 8 to 10 segments while still warm, then cut when completely cold.

blueberry-pecan bran muffins

THE MIXTURE WILL BE SLIGHTLY WETTER THAN YOU EXPECT, BUT THE BRAN WILL ABSORB THE EXTRA MOISTURE. **MAKES 6**

¼ cup (60 mL) butter

1 large egg, beaten

½ cup (125 mL) milk

¼ cup (60 mL) light brown sugar

¾ cup (175 mL) whole-wheat flour

½ cup (125 mL) bran

1½ tsp (7 mL) baking powder

¾ cup (175 mL) blueberries

⅓ cup (90 mL) pecans, finely chopped

1 Preheat the oven to 400°F (200°C) and double-line 6 large muffin cups with paper cups. Melt the butter and leave it to cool slightly. Beat the egg with the milk, add the sugar, and leave to stand.

2 Mix all the dry ingredients together in a bowl and add the blueberries and chopped nuts. Mix the butter with the milk and egg, then pour into the bowl and mix quickly and lightly – this should take no more than a few seconds. Do not beat the mixture, which will seem rather wet.

3 Divide the mixture among the 6 prepared muffin cups and bake immediately in the preheated oven for 30 minutes. Cool briefly on a wire rack and serve warm.

zucchini and raisin cake

A MOIST VERSION OF THE CONVENTIONAL CARROT CAKE. **MAKES 1 LARGE CAKE**

1⅔ cups (400 mL) whole-wheat flour

1 tsp (5 mL) baking soda

2 tsp (10 mL) baking powder

1 tsp (5 mL) ground ginger

1 cup (250 mL) soft brown sugar

⅔ cup (150 mL) raisins

1 cup (250 mL) grated zucchini, closely packed

1 cup (250 mL) grated carrot

⅔ cup (150 mL) plain yogurt

3 large eggs, beaten

⅔ cup (150 mL) corn oil

1 Preheat the oven to 350°F (175°C), and line a 9-in (23-cm) round cake pan with baking parchment.

2 Place the flour, baking soda, baking powder, ginger, sugar, and raisins in a bowl, then mix in the zucchini and carrot. Add the yogurt with the eggs, then finally add the oil. Mix to a thick batter and beat vigorously for 1 minute. Pour the mixture into the prepared pan, and bake in the preheated oven for 1 hour, until a toothpick inserted into the mixture comes out clean. Cool slightly, then turn out onto a wire rack and leave to cool.

granola cake

THIS IS BEST STORED FOR 2 TO 3 DAYS BEFORE EATING. **MAKES 1 CAKE**

1½ cups (375 mL) granola

½ cup (125 mL) light brown sugar

⅓ cup (90 mL) liquid honey

1 cup (250 mL) golden raisins

1 cup (250 mL) unsweetened grape or orange juice

1 cup (250 mL) whole-wheat flour

2 tsp (10 mL) baking powder

1 tsp (5 mL) baking soda

2 tsp (10 mL) pumpkin pie spice (see p. 200)

1 large egg, beaten

1 Preheat the oven to 325°F (160°C), then grease and line a 7 x 11-in (18 x 28-cm) cake pan. Heat the granola, sugar, honey, and raisins with the fruit juice until the sugar has dissolved; leave to cool for 10 minutes.

2 Mix together the dry ingredients. Add the beaten egg to the granola mix, then add the dry ingredients and quickly beat into a thick, frothy paste. Pour into the prepared cake pan, lightly smooth the top, and bake in the preheated oven for 40 minutes. Cool slightly, then mark into squares. Allow to cool completely on a wire rack before cutting to store in an airtight container.

honeyed ginger cake

THE HONEY MAKES THIS MILDER THAN MOST GINGER CAKES.

MAKES 1 LOAF CAKE

½ **cup (125 mL) margarine or butter**

½ **cup (125 mL) honey**

½ **cup (125 mL) light brown sugar**

2 **cups (500 mL) whole-wheat flour**

1½ **tsp (7 mL) baking soda**

2 **tsp (10 mL) ground ginger**

2 **large eggs, beaten**

2 **Tbsp (25 mL) milk**

1 Preheat the oven to 325°F (160°C) and line an 11 x 7-in (28 x 18-cm) pan with baking parchment.

2 Heat the margarine, honey, and sugar together over low heat until the margarine has melted and the sugar dissolved – do not allow the mixture to boil or the cake will become crusty. Remove from the heat and leave to cool.

3 Mix the dry ingredients together in a large bowl and make a well in the center. Beat the eggs with the milk and stir into the honey mixture. Add to the dry ingredients and mix thoroughly. Pour into the prepared pan and bake in the preheated oven for 40 minutes, or until a toothpick inserted into the cake comes out clean. Remove from the pan and cool completely on a wire rack. Wrap in foil or store in an airtight container for 1 to 2 days to allow the flavor to develop before eating. Drizzle with icing if you like.

date squares

THIS CAKE IS DELICIOUS BUT IS HIGH IN CALORIES, SO IS BEST FOR OCCASIONAL
TREATS. **SERVES 8 TO 10**

2 cups (500 mL) dates, chopped

⅔ cup (125 mL) water

1 tsp (10 mL) vanilla extract

¾ cup (175 mL) butter

2 cups (500 mL) rolled oats

1 cup (250 mL) whole-wheat flour

1 cup (250 mL) light brown sugar

1 Preheat the oven to 350°F (175°C) and line a deep 8-in (20-cm) baking pan. Place the dates and water in a saucepan and cook slowly until the dates are soft, the water is slightly reduced, and the mixture can be beaten into a thick purée. Add the vanilla and set the mixture aside until needed.

2 Melt the butter in a saucepan, then stir in the remaining ingredients. Press half the mixture into the bottom of the prepared pan, then top it with the date mixture and then the remaining oat mixture. Smooth the top, then bake in the preheated oven for 30 minutes.

3 Mark into portions while still warm, then leave to cool completely before slicing. Store in an airtight container.

pineapple raisin cake

AN EVERYDAY FRUIT CAKE, EMBELLISHED WITH UNUSUAL DRIED FRUIT. **MAKES 1 MEDIUM CAKE**

1 cup (250 mL) dried mixed fruit (pineapple, golden raisins, dried cranberries, etc.)

½ cup (125 mL) pineapple or orange juice

¾ cup (175 mL) margarine or butter

2 cups (500 mL) whole-wheat flour

2 tsp (10 mL) baking powder

Pinch of salt

1 tsp (5 mL) ground ginger

½ cup (125 mL) light brown sugar

2 large eggs, beaten

1 Soak the fruit in the fruit juice for 10 minutes. Preheat the oven to 350°F (175°C) and lightly grease a deep 7-in (18-cm) round cake pan.

2 Blend the butter into the flour, baking powder, salt, and ginger in a bowl until the mixture resembles fine bread crumbs. Stir in the sugar, then add the fruits and juice and the beaten eggs. Mix to smooth batter adding a little extra fruit juice or milk as required, then spoon the mixture into the prepared cake pan.

3 Bake in the preheated oven for 1¼ hours, or until the cake stops "singing" – yes, go on, listen to it – and a toothpick inserted into the center comes out clean.

4 Cool slightly in the pan, then turn out carefully onto a wire rack to cool completely.

cranberry coffee cake

A LIGHT SPONGE CAKE TO SERVE PLAIN OR WITH CREAM AND FRUITS. **MAKES 1 CAKE**

3 large eggs

½ cup (125 mL) light brown sugar

⅔ cup (150 mL) whole-wheat flour

1 Tbsp (15 mL) sunflower oil

1 tsp (5 mL) coffee flavoring or very strong cold espresso coffee

⅓ cup (90 mL) dried cranberries, chopped

1 Preheat the oven to 375°F (190°C) then lightly grease an 8- to 9-in (20- to 23-cm) cake pan and line the base with baking parchment.

2 Whisk the eggs and sugar together until pale and fluffy – this is best done in an electric mixer and may take up to 10 minutes. Fold in the flour a few spoonfuls at a time, then add the oil and coffee, drizzling them down the side of the bowl. Finally, add the cranberries, folding in lightly. Transfer the mixture immediately to the prepared cake pan and bake in the preheated oven for 20 to 25 minutes, until the mixture springs back when pressed lightly and shrinks away from the sides of the tin.

3 Turn the cake out onto a wire rack to cool completely. Decorate with fruit and whipped cream, if wished, then serve sliced.

carrot cake

I AM VERY GENEROUS WITH THE FROSTING ON THIS WONDERFUL CAKE
– YOU CAN'T BE GOOD ALL THE TIME! **MAKES 1 LARGE CAKE**

2 cups (500 mL) whole-wheat flour

2 tsp (10 mL) baking powder

1 tsp (5 mL) baking soda

1 tsp (5 mL) salt

1 tsp (5 mL) pumpkin pie spice (optional) (see p. 200)

½ cup (125 mL) walnut pieces, finely chopped

3 large eggs, beaten

**⅔ cup (150 mL) mashed ripe banana
(about 2 medium)**

1½ cups (375 mL) grated carrot

¾ cup (175 mL) sunflower oil

FROSTING

¾ cup (175 mL) softened unsalted butter

¾ cup (175 mL) cream cheese

1 tsp (5 mL) vanilla extract

2½ cups (375 mL) icing sugar, sieved

1 Preheat the oven to 350°F (175°C) then lightly grease a deep 9-in (23-cm) round cake pan and line it with baking parchment.

2 Mix all the dry ingredients together in a large bowl, then add the eggs, mashed bananas, and carrots. Pour the oil into the bowl and beat thoroughly to a thick, well-blended batter. Spoon into the prepared cake pan and bake in the center of the preheated oven for about 1 hour, until a toothpick inserted into the cake comes out clean. Remove the cake carefully from the cake pan and allow to cool completely on a wire rack.

3 Prepare the frosting by beating together the softened butter and cream cheese until blended into the frosting, then add the vanilla essence and beat again. Sift the icing sugar and beat it gradually into the cheese mixture. Spread the frosting over the cooled cake and decorate, if wished, with finely chopped walnuts or a little extra grated carrot. Serve in thin slices.

rhubarb streusel cake

THE TOPPING GIVES A DELICIOUS CRUNCH IN CONTRAST TO THE MOIST RHUBARB. **MAKES 1 LARGE CAKE**

STREUSEL TOPPING

⅓ **cup (90 mL) butter**

1 cup (250 mL) whole-wheat flour

½ **tsp (2 mL) baking powder**

½ **cup (125 mL) Demerara sugar**

½ **cup (125 mL) butter or margarine**

⅔ **cup (150 mL) light brown sugar**

2 large eggs, beaten

1 cup (250 mL) whole-wheat flour

1 tsp (5 mL) baking powder

½ **tsp (2 mL) cinnamon**

1 Tbsp (15 mL) milk

**2 cups (500 mL) rhubarb pieces, in
    2-in (5-cm) lengths, fresh or canned**

1 Preheat the oven to 350°F (175°C), then line a deep 8-in (20-cm) round cake pan with baking parchment.

2 First prepare the topping. Blend the butter into the flour, baking powder, and sugar until evenly distributed, then set aside. Cream the butter and sugar together until pale and fluffy, then gradually add the beaten eggs. Mix the flour, baking powder, and cinnamon together and fold it into the mixture, adding the milk to make a smooth batter.

3 Spoon the cake mixture into the prepared pan. Arrange the rhubarb over the cake and cover with the topping mixture, spreading it evenly.

4 Bake the cake in the preheated oven for 1 hour, or until a toothpick inserted into the cake comes out clean. Leave in the pan for 2 to 3 minutes, then remove the cake carefully, peel off the paper, and allow to cool completely on a wire rack.

oat squares

SIMILAR TO GINGERBREAD IN TASTE, WITH A ROUGHER TEXTURE. DON'T LET THE MOLASSES BOIL OR YOU WILL GET A TOUGH CRUST. **MAKES 1 CAKE**

¾ cup (175 mL) molasses

⅓ cup (150 mL) light brown sugar

½ cup (125 mL) margarine or butter

1¼ cups (375 mL) whole-wheat flour

2 tsp (10 mL) baking powder

Pinch of salt

1 cup (250 mL) steel-cut or Irish oatmeal

2 large eggs, beaten

About ⅔ cup (150 mL) milk to mix

1 Preheat the oven to 325°F (160°C) and line an 11 x 7-in (28 x 18-cm) pan with baking parchment.

2 Heat the molasses, sugar, and margarine gently until the margarine has melted and the sugar has dissolved. Leave to cool slightly. Mix all the dry ingredients together in a large bowl and make a well in the center. Add the beaten eggs to the liquid and pour into the dry ingredients; mix thoroughly, adding sufficient milk to give a soft, runny consistency.

3 Pour the batter quickly into the prepared pan and bake in the preheated oven for 1 hour. Carefully transfer onto a wire rack to cool. Cut into squares when cold and store in an airtight container until required.

whole-wheat cinnamon cookies

PERFECT FOR DUNKING IN COFFEE OR HOT CHOCOLATE. **MAKES 18**

¼ cup (60 mL) butter

1 cup (250 mL) whole-wheat flour

½ tsp (6 mL) nutmeg

⅔ cup (150 mL) soft brown sugar

1 medium egg, beaten

2 Tbsp (25 mL) Demerara sugar

1 tsp (5 mL) cinnamon

1 Blend the butter into the flour, nutmeg, and brown sugar, then bind to a dough with the beaten egg. Turn out onto a floured surface and knead lightly until the dough is smooth. Cover in plastic wrap and chill for at least 30 minutes.

2 Preheat the oven to 400°F (200°C). Shape into 18 walnut-sized pieces, then place on greased cookie sheets and flatten slightly with a fork. Mix together the Demerara sugar and cinnamon, and sprinkle the mixture over the cookies. Bake for 12 to 15 minutes, swapping the trays halfway through cooking if necessary so they cook evenly. Cool on a wire rack and store in an airtight tin.

apricot granola bars

THESE FRUIT GRANOLA BARS MAKE FOR A SUBSTANTIAL SNACK OR EVEN A LIGHT MEAL SUBSTITUTE. **MAKES 8**

FILLING

1 cup (250 mL) dried apricots, finely chopped

Grated rind and juice of 1 medium orange

⅓ cup (90 mL) margarine or butter

⅓ cup (90 mL) honey

2 cups (500 mL) granola

½ cup (125 mL) whole-wheat flour

1 Preheat the oven to 375°F (190°C) and lightly grease a 7-in (18-cm) square cake pan.

2 Cook the apricots with the orange rind and juice, simmering slowly until all the orange juice has disappeared. Allow to cool. Melt the margarine in a saucepan, add the honey, and heat gently until melted into the margarine. Stir in the granola and flour and mix well.

3 Press half the granola mixture into the prepared cake pan, then cover with a layer of apricots. Top with the remaining granola mixture, pressing it down and smoothing the top with a metal spoon. Try to poke any raisins into the mixture so that they do not burn.

4 Bake in the preheated oven for 20 to 25 minutes, until lightly browned. Mark into bars and allow to cool in the pan. Cut through, then cool completely on a wire rack. Store in an airtight container.

ABOVE PEANUT BUTTER COOKIES

granola cookies

CHILL THE MIXTURE BEFORE BAKING OR THE COOKIES WILL SPREAD TOO MUCH IN
THE OVEN. **MAKES ABOUT 20**

½ cup (125 mL) butter or margarine

½ cup (125 mL) light brown sugar

¼ cup (60 mL) honey

2 cups (500 mL) low-fat granola

½ cup (125 mL) whole-wheat flour

1 Cream the butter and sugar together until pale and fluffy, then add the honey and beat thoroughly again. Work in the granola and flour to give a stiff dough that is only slightly sticky, then turn out onto a lightly floured surface and knead firmly until the dough is easily manageable. Form into a sausage shape, about 12 in (30 cm) long, then cover in plastic wrap and chill in the refrigerator for at least 30 minutes.

2 Preheat the oven to 350°F (175°C) and lightly grease 2 baking sheets. Cut the cookie dough into 20 pieces, form into balls, then flatten slightly and place on the prepared baking sheets. Bake in the preheated oven for 12 to 15 minutes, until lightly browned. Leave the cookies to cool slightly on the baking sheets until firm enough to transfer to a wire rack to cool completely. Store in an airtight container or cookie jar.

peanut butter cookies

BEWARE, THESE COOKIES ARE RICH! **MAKES 18**

⅓ cup (90 mL) crunchy peanut butter

¼ cup (60 mL) margarine

½ cup (125 mL) Demerara sugar

1 large egg, beaten

1 cup (250 mL) whole-wheat flour

1 tsp (5 mL) baking powder

1 Cream together the peanut butter, margarine, and sugar, then add the beaten egg. Fold in the flour and baking powder and form into a stiff dough. Turn out onto a floured surface and knead lightly. Cover in plastic wrap and chill for about 1½ hours, until firmer and easier to handle.

2 Preheat the oven to 350°F (175°C) and lightly grease 2 baking sheets. Cut the dough into 18 slices and form each into a ball, then press lightly to flatten as you place them on the prepared baking sheets. Dip a fork into a little flour and press it into the tops of the cookies, then bake in the preheated oven for 15 to 20 minutes. Cool slightly before transferring to a wire rack to cool completely.

all-butter shortbread

BUTTER IS ESSENTIAL TO GIVE THIS COOKIE THE MOST DELICIOUS FLAVOR. **MAKES 1 LARGE SHORTBREAD**

½ cup (125 mL) slightly softened
   unsalted butter

1 cup (250 mL) whole-wheat flour,
   fine if available

Pinch of salt

⅓ cup (90 mL) light brown sugar

1 Preheat the oven to 350°F (175°C) and lightly grease a 7-in (18-cm) baking pan – I usually line the pan with baking parchment, although this is not essential.

2 Blend the butter into the flour, salt, and sugar in a bowl until the mixture resembles fine bread crumbs. Turn into the prepared pan and press down with a broad-bladed knife. Lightly mark the shortbread into 8 portions, then prick through to the base using a fork and make a decorative edge.

3 Bake in the preheated oven for 25 to 30 minutes. Cool slightly in the pan, then mark the shortbread into portions again before turning out onto a wire rack to cool. Cut through or break into portions when completely cooled.

walnut cookies

IF YOU PREFER, COAT THE COOKIES IN MELTED CHOCOLATE ONCE THEY HAVE COOLED. **MAKES ABOUT 30**

½ cup (125 mL) unsalted butter,
  slightly softened

⅔ cup (150 mL) light brown sugar

1 large egg, beaten

1 cup (250 mL) whole-wheat flour

1 tsp (5 mL) baking powder

¾ cup (175 mL) walnut pieces, finely
  chopped

1 Cream the butter and sugar together until pale – the mixture will be slightly sticky. Add the egg and mix well, fold in the flour and baking powder, then finally work in the nuts.

2 Turn the mixture out onto a lightly floured surface and knead gently to bring the dough together. Roll into a sausage shape about 12 in (30 cm) long, wrap in plastic wrap, and chill for at least 1 hour, until firm enough to handle.

3 Preheat the oven to 350°F (175°C) and lightly grease 2 or 3 baking sheets. Cut the dough into thin slices and roll them into balls about the size of a walnut. Place on the prepared baking sheets, flattening the cookies slightly with the palm of your hand. Bake for 12 to 15 minutes, then allow to cool slightly on the baking sheet before transferring to a wire rack to cool completely.

Index

Adzuki and Fennel Casserole 128
All-Butter Shortbread 220
Apple Bean Betty 163
Apple Cake, Danish 177
Apple Ratatouille with Spiced
    Pork 142
Apples, Stuffed Baked 176
Apricot, Almond and Tomato
    Salad 80
Apricot Bread
Apricot Cheesecake 156
Apricot Granola Bars 216
Apricots, Fresh, with Dried
    Cherries and Ginger 164
Armenian Soup 41
Artichoke and Corn Soup 28
Atholl Brose 174

Baked Bananas with Rum 158
Banana Bran Custard 152
Banana Bread, pear and 184
Banana Cornmeal Muffins 204
Banana and Rhubarb Trifle 164
Bananas with Rum, Baked 158
Barley and Rye Bread 182
beans, varieties of 19ñ20
Beans
    Adzuki and Fennel Casserole 128
    Apple Bean Betty 163
    Baby Lima Bean and Tuna
        Salad 76
    Bean and Vegetable
        Turnovers 112
    Cassoulet 132
    Chicken and Bean Chowder 48
    Chicken and Flageolet Bean
        Risotto 134
    Chicken and Kidney Bean
        Gumbo 130
    Chicken and Lima Bean
        Bourguignon 129
    Lima Bean and Parsnip
        Chowder 32
    Mexican Bean Soup 41
    Navy Beans with Broccoli 117
    Pasta Primavera 106
    Pasta Salad 60

    Quick Bean Pot 113
    Spiced Baked Beans 115
    Vegetable Tortillas with Mixed
Bean Salsa 102
    Warm Jalapeño Bean Dip 83
Beef, Thai-style 146
Beet and Sorrel Salad 70
Beet Soup with Horseradish 38
Blueberry-Pecan Bran Muffins 205
Bran Bread 192
Brazil Nut Loaf 104
Brie Quesadillas 83
Broccoli Soup 35
Brown Rice Salad with Fruit and
    Seeds 66
Buckwheat and Mushroom Soup 52
Buckwheat Salad 66
Buns, Spiced Fruit 202
Buns, Sticky 200

Caramelized Onion Tart 126
Carrot Cake 212
Carrot Pudding 162
Cassoulet 132
Cauliflower and Cumin Soup,
    Cream of 32
cereals and grains, varieties of 12-16
Chapatis 193
Cheese
    Apricot Cheesecake 156
    Brie Quesadillas 83
    Cheese and Walnut Scone
        Rounds 199
    Chestnut and Blue Cheese
        Soup 36
    Date and Pear Cottage
        Cheese Salad 70
    Glamorgan Sausages 118
    Nut and Cream Cheese
        Peppers 84
    Pasta Salad 60
    Pumpkin and Cheese Bread 183
    Ratatouille and Goat Cheese
        Quiche 111
    Stuffed Anaheim Chiles 95
    Whole-wheat Cheese Rolls 193
Chestnut and Blue Cheese Soup 36

Chestnut and Cranberry
    Casserole 122
Chicken and Bean Chowder 48
Chicken with Cabbage, Spiced 137
Chicken and Flageolet Bean
    Risotto 134
Chicken Chowder, Thai-spiced 47
Chicken and Kidney Bean
    Gumbo 130
Chicken and Lima Bean
    Bourguignon 129
Chicken and Sweet Potato
    Curry 133
Chicken and Vegetable
    Fricassee 132
Chickpea Soup with Red Pepper
    Salsa 54
Chickpeas with Sesame Sauce 100
Chickpeas, Spiced Lamb with 144
Classic Waldorf Salad 62
Cookies, Granola 219
    Peanut Butter 219
    Walnut 221
    Whole-wheat Cinnamon 215
Corn Mexicali 100
Corn Salad, Crunchy 64
Cornbread, Creamed Corn 194
    Molasses 196
Couscous Salad, Summer 73
Couscous Soup, Lebanese 47
Crab Balls with Sweet Lime
    Sauce 97
Crab with Ginger and Grapefruit 96
Crab and Sweet Corn Soup 52
Cracked Wheat Pilaf 120
Cracked Wheat Salad 68
Cranberry Coffee Cake 211
Cream of Cauliflower and Cumin
    Soup 32
Creamed Corn Cornbread 194
Crunchy Corn Salad 64
Cucumber Tabbouleh 67
Curried Lentil Soufflé 112
Curried Vegetable Casserole 118

Danish Apple Cake 177
Date and Ginger Pudding 159

Date and pear Cottage Cheese
    Salad 70
Date Squares 210
Deviled Leek Crostini 92 162
Drop Scones, Whole-wheat 199

Eggs
    Curried Lentil Soufflé 112
    New Potatoes Niçoise 71
    Peanut and Bean Sprout
        Risotto 123
    Ratatouille and Goat Cheese
        Quiche 111
    Spinach and Walnut Whole-wheat
        Quiche 108
Eggplant Pâté 90
Endive and Pink Grapefruit Salad,
    Roasted 62

Fennel and Walnut Soup 40
fiber, importance of 7
Fig Cake 204
Fig and Pecan Pie 168
Fish
    Flageolet and Tuna Salad 76
    Smoked Fish Chowder 50
    Spanish-style Haddock 140
    Stir-fried Trout 140
    Trout with Wild Rice
        Stuffing 138
Flageolet and Tuna Salad 76
French Onion Soup 30
Fresh Apricots with Dried Cherries
    and Ginger 164

Gazpacho 42
Glamorgan Sausages 118
Golden Raisin Scones 198
Granola Cake 206
Granola Cookies 219
Guacamole 95

Haddock, Spanish-style 140
Hazelnut and Zucchini Pasta 105
Honeyed Ginger Cake 208
Hummus 90

Ice Cream, Rum and Raisin
        Yogurt 152
    Vanilla 153

Lamb with Chickpeas, Spiced 144
Lamb with Lentils and Prunes 141
Lebanese Couscous Soup 47
Leek Crostini, Deviled 92
Leek and Spinach Barley Soup 56
Lentils
    Armenian Soup 41
    Curried Lentil Soufflé 112
    Lamb with Lentils and
        Prunes 141
    Lentils and Rice 117
    Lentil Salad 73
    Minestrone 44
    Stuffed Anaheim Chiles 95
    Tomato, Orange and Lentil
        Soup 36
Light Rye Sourdough 187
Lima Bean and Parsnip Chowder 32

Malted Grain Bread 190
Mango Yogurt Brulée 158
Meringues, Pineapple Oat 168
Mexican Bean Soup 41
Mincemeat and Apple Tart 169
Millet Rounds with Yogurt
    Sauce 121
Millet and Vegetable Gratin 111
Minestrone 44
Minted Pea Soup 33
Molasses Cornbread 196
Mousse, Prune and Brandy 174
Muffins, Banana Cornmeal 204
    Blueberry-Pecan Bran 205
Mulligatawny Soup 44
Mushrooms
    Brazil Nut Loaf 104
    Buckwheat and Mushroom
        Soup 52
    Mushroom and Hazelnut Pâté 78
    Stuffed Zucchini with Tomato
        Sauce 96
    Wild Rice Casserole 122
    Wild Rice-stuffed Mushrooms 78

New Potatoes Niçoise 71
Nutbread Loaves 188
Nuts
    Blueberry-Pecan Bran
        Muffins 205
    Brazil Nut Loaf 104

Cheese and Walnut Scone
    Rounds 199
Classic Waldorf Salad 62
Fennel and Walnut Soup 40
Hazelnut and Zucchini Pasta 105
Mushroom and Hazelnut Pâté 76
Nut and Cream Cheese
    Peppers 84
Nutbread Loaves 188
Prune and Walnut Tart 157
Quick Onion and Nut Loaf 189
Spinach and Walnut Whole-wheat
    Quiche 108
Toasted Hazelnut Rye Bread 182
Walnut Cookies 221

Oat Squares 215
Onion and Nut Loaf, Quick 189
Onion Soup, French 30
Onion Tart, Caramelized 126
Orange Breakfast Bread, spiced 186
Orange and Butternut Soup 26
Orange and Golden Raisin Rice
    Pudding 176

Pancakes, Tangerine and Cream
    Cheese 173
Parsnip and Apple Soup 29
Pasta
    Hazelnut and Zucchini Pasta 105
    Lentil and Pumpkin Lasagne 101
    Minestrone 44
    Pasta Primavera 106
    Pasta Salad 60
    Sausage, Apple and Pasta Soup 28
Pastry
    Bean and Vegetable
        Turnovers 112
    Caramelized Onion Tart 126
    Fig and Pecan Pie 168
    Mincemeat and Apple Tart 169
    Prune and Walnut Tart 157
    Ratatouille and Goat Cheese
        Quiche 111
    Roasted Tomato Tartlets 85
    Spinach and Walnut Whole-wheat
        Quiche 108
Pâté, Eggplant 90
    Mushroom and Hazelnut 78
Pea Soup, Minted 33

Peanut and Bean Sprout Risotto 123
Peanut Butter Cookies 219
Pear and Banana Bread 184
Pear and Grape Salad 63

Pineapple with Apricots and
    Berries 166
Pineapple Oat Meringues 168
Pineapple Raisin Cake 210
Pizzas, Quick-bake Calabrian 86
Plum and Apple Pudding 150
Pork
    Apple Ratatouille with Spiced
        Pork 142
Potato Griddle Scones 188
Prune and Brandy Mousse 174
Prune and Walnut Tart 157
Pumpkin and Carrot Soup 35
Pumpkin and Cheese Bread 183
Pumpkin Lasagne, Lentil and 101
Pumpkin and Smoked Mussel Soup,
    Roasted 55

Quick-bake Calabrian Pizzas 86
Quick Bean Pot 113
Quick Bran Teabread 203
Quick Onion and Nut Loaf 189

Rhubarb Streusel Cake 214
rice, varieties and uses of 16ñ17
Rice
    Brown Rice Salad with Fruit and
        Seeds 66
    Chicken and Flageolet Bean
        Risotto 134
    Lentils and Rice 117
    Orange and Golden Raisin
        Rice Pudding 176
    Peanut and Bean Sprout
        Risotto 123
    Rice and Pistachio Salad 74
    Spinach and Pancetta Risotto 115
    Sweet Fruit Pilaf and Butter
        Pudding 154
    Wild Rice Casserole 122
    Wild Rice Quick Bread 190
    Wild Rice-stuffed Mushrooms 78
Roasted Endive and Pink Grapefruit
    Salad 62
Roasted Pumpkin and Smoked
    Mussel Soup 55

Roasted Tomato Tartlets 85
Rum and Raisin Yogurt Ice
    Cream 152
Rye Bread, Barley and 182
Rye Bread, Toasted Hazelnut 182
Rye Sourdough, Light 187

Sausage, Apple and Pasta Soup 28
Scone Rounds, Cheese and
    Walnut 199
Scones, Golden Raisin 198
    Potato Griddle 188
Shortbread, All-Butter 220
Shrimp Chow Mein 137
Smoked Fish Chowder 50
Soda Bread 187
Soft Fruits with Lime
    Mascarpone 178
Sourdough, Light Rye 187
Spanish-style Haddock 140
Spiced Baked Beans 115
Spiced Berry Pudding 172
Spiced Chicken with Cabbage 137
Spiced Fruit Buns 202
Spiced Lamb with Chickpeas 144
Spiced Orange Breakfast Bread 186
Spiced Vegetables with Yogurt 89
Spinach and Pancetta Risotto 115
Spinach Salad 72
Spinach and Walnut Whole-wheat
    Quiche 108
Spinach and Zucchini Soup 40
Squash
    Orange and Butternut Soup 26
    Squash Chowder 49
Sticky Buns 200
Stir-fried Trout 104
Strawberries with Melon and
    Orange 165
Strawberry and Orange Trifle 157
Stuffed Anaheim Chiles 95
Stuffed Baked Apples 176
Stuffed Zucchini with Tomato
    Sauce 96
Summer Couscous Salad 73
Summer Fruit Upside-down
    Trifle 170
Sweet Fruit Pilaf 162
Sweet and Sour Vegetable
    Stir-fry 124

Tangerine and Cream Cheese
    Pancakes 173
Teabread, Quick Bran 203
Thai-spiced Chicken Chowder 47
Thai-style Beef 146
Toasted Hazelnut Rye Bread 182
Tomatoes
    Apricot, Almond and Tomato
        Salad 80
    Gazpacho 42
    Roasted Tomato Tartlets 85
    Tomato, Orange and Lentil
        Soup 36
Tortilla Wheels with Pineapple
    Salsa 79
Trifle, Banana and Rhubarb 164
    Strawberry and Orange 157
    Summer Fruit Upside-down 170
Trout, Stir-fried 140
Trout with Wild Rice Stuffing 138

Vanilla Ice Cream 153
Vegetable Casserole, Curried 118
Vegetable Stir-fry, Sweet and
    Sour 124
Vegetable Tortillas with Mixed Bean
    Salsa 102
Vegetables with Yogurt, Spiced 89

Walnut Cookies 221
Warm Jalapeño Bean Dip 83
Warm Spiced Compote 160
Whole-wheat Cheese Rolls 193
Whole-wheat Cinnamon
    Cookies 215
Whole-wheat Drop scones 199
Whole-wheat Honey and Pecan
    Bread 202
Whole-wheat Morning Rolls 197
Whole-wheat Sandwich Loaf 196
Wild Rice Casserole 122
Wild Rice Quick Bread 190
Wild Rice-stuffed Mushrooms 78

Zucchini Pasta, Hazelnut and 105
Zucchini and Raisin Cake 206
Zucchini with Tomato Sauce,
    Stuffed 96

I dedicate this book with love to

my mother,
Charlotte

from whom I inherited my language and music ability, who exposed me to classical music all through my childhood (over my protests!), and who yelled at me to "Practice that piano!"

*It paid off, Ma.
Thanks.*

CONTENTS

PRELUDE
    A Tribute to WFOS-FM   xi
    Other Acknowledgments   xii
OVERTURE
    Why This Guide?   xiii
    The Old "Native vs. Anglicized" Controversy   xiv
    Caveat Dictor   xv
    Structure of the Book   xvi
    Suggestions for Using The Book   xvii
    Limitations   xviii
MOVEMENT 1. TRANSCRIPTION AND OTHER BASICS   1
Transcription Conventions   1
    Letter vs. Sound   1
    Options and Alternatives   3
    Which Phonetic Transcription?   4
    Is the Glass Half-Full or Half-Empty?   4
Sound Symbols   5
    Vowels   5
    Consonants   9
How to Read the Lists   12
    On Alphabetical Order   12
What's in a Name?   15
    People and Places   15
    Of Firsts and Lasts   18
    Language, Ethnicity, Religion, and Politics   18
    More on Slash Designations   20
MOVEMENT 2. ALPHABETICAL LIST   21
MOVEMENT 3. LIST BY LANGUAGE   112
Armenian   112
Bulgarian   112
Chinese   113
Czech and the Haček Languages   113
    (Slovak, Serbo-Croatian, Slovenian,
    Lithuanian, Latvian)
    Note on Last Names   113

Dutch and Flemish   116
English   119
Finnish and Estonian   128
French   128
German   137
Greek   148
Hungarian   149
Italian   151
Japanese   161
Korean   161
Latin   161
Polish   162
     Note on Polish Last Names   162
Portuguese   164
Romanian   165
Russian and Ukrainian   165
Scandinavian (Danish, Norwegian, Swedish)   168
Spanish   169
FIVE INTERLUDES FOR TONGUE AND LARYNX   173
Interlude 1. The Voicing Principle   173
     Two Kinds of Consonants   173
Interlude 2. Consonants on Paper and in the Mouth   175
     Some Terminology for Types of Sounds   176
     So-called Hard and Soft Consonants   177
     Flap, Catch, Shift   179
     Doubles and Dub Bulls   182
     Consonant Cluster Reprise   183
Interlude 3. Vowels in "General European" vs. English   184
     Vowels in the Mouth   184
     Other Vowel Sounds   184
     Of Diphthongs and Digraphs   185
     "Long" and "Short"   185
     "Broad" and "Flat"   186
     Shwa   186
Interlude 4. Stress Management   187
Interlude 5. Hints on Reading Key Signatures   189
MOVEMENT 4. LETTER AND SOUND IN THE LANGUAGES
OF EUROPE AND EAST ASIA   191
General Remark on Accent Marks and Diacritics   191
Romance Languages   192
     Latin   192
     Italian   193
     Romanian   196

French 197

Portuguese 200

Spanish 202

Germanic Languages 205

English 205

German 208

Two Notes on Visual Impressions 208

Note on Names, Letters, and Immigration 210

Voicing Reprise 212

Dutch and Flemish 213

Scandinavian (Danish, Norwegian, Swedish) 216

Slavic and Baltic Languages 217

On Language, Religion, and Alphabet 218

Polish 218

The Haček Languages 222
(Czech, Slovak, Serbo-Croatian, Slovenian;
Lithuanian, Latvian)

Russian-Ukrainian-Bulgarian 224

A Guide to Russian Last and Middle Names 228

Finno-Ugric and Other European Languages 230

Finnish, Estonian, Hungarian 230

From the Ends of Europe 232

Albanian, Greek 232

Turkish, Welsh, Irish 233

East Asian Languages 233

Japanese and Korean 234

Japanese Stress and Vowel Skipping 234

Chinese 234

CODA 236

Diacritic Review 236

Letter-to-Sound Review 238

Sound-to-Letter Review 239

The Palatal Challenge 240

FINALE. ANNOTATED BIBLIOGRAPHY 241

I. Names but no phonetics 241

II. Names *and* phonetics 244

III. General Transcription, Phonetics for Singers, etc. 250

INDEXES 253